Soviet Marxism

SOVIET MARXISM

A

CRITICAL ANALYSIS

BY

Herbert Marcuse

VINTAGE BOOKS

A Division of Random House

NEW YORK

PREFACE TO
THE VINTAGE EDITION

1961

The reception of this book was a strange one. In the Soviet Union, critics accused me of endeavoring "to deprecate and distort communist morality," to consider "capitalist society as the triumph of individual freedom," and to repeat "the old bourgeois lie about socialism being a rigorous totalitarian system based on universal oppression." In the United States, I am said to treat "Soviet Marxism as a stage in mankind's struggle toward freedom and socialism," and to be more unambiguous in my "critical analysis of Western life and society" than in my analysis of the Soviet Union. I take these contradictions as suggesting that I have achieved a modicum of success in freeing myself from Cold War propaganda and in presenting a relatively objective analysis based on a reasoned interpretation of historical developments.

I should like to use the limited space of this preface for referring my interpretation of Soviet Marxism to some of the major events which occurred after the date of publication.

The trend toward reform and liberalization within the Soviet Union has continued. Administrative de centralization, emphasis on legality as against incal culable arbitrariness, shift in the enforcement o military discipline from brutality to "persuasion," greater range of freedom for writers, artists, and critics, and, most important, gradual introduction of a reduced working day and increasing availability of consumer goods testify to this trend. An American expert whom nobody could in fairness accuse o sympathy writes after a devastating denunciation o the persistence of totalitarianism in the Soviet Union

To use a historical simile, Khrushchev's era has mean the introduction of enlightened totalitarianism in the USSR and a conscious effort to dispense with the patholog ical, uneconomic, and plainly unnecessary aspects of to talitarianism inherited from Stalin.[1]

In his courageous and sober book *The Great Contest* Isaac Deutscher has recently reviewed and evaluated the Soviet developments of the last years in the international context. It is only in this context, and in their interrelation with Western developments that they can be properly analyzed.

At the outset, recent Soviet foreign policy appears to refute the hypothesis of tendential liberalization The collapse of the summit conference in May 1960 and the intransigent attitude of the Soviet delegation in the United Nations seem to mark clearly enough the return to a "hard" policy. Moreover, the declara tion of the Representatives of Communist and Work ers' Parties at the Congress of the Rumanian Workers Party in Bucharest in June 1960 was interpreted in the American press as re-emphasizing "revolution

[1] Adam B. Ulam: "The New Face of Soviet Totalitarianism," *World Politics*, Vol. XII, No. 3 (April 1960), p. 410.

by non-peaceful means," in contrast with the Moscow declaration of 1957—a shift in emphasis which was explained as a Soviet concession to Chinese objections against the line of "peaceful coexistence." I propose to discuss briefly these events.

It might be well to start with the Soviet–Chinese controversy on the political value of "peaceful co-existence." The controversy has been almost universally presented in terms of the "inevitability of war between the imperialist and socialist countries." In contrast to the Chinese, the Soviets are reiterating that the international constellation of power has, since Lenin, changed to such an extent that the Leninist thesis on the inevitability of conflict is no longer valid. "To be sure, the essence of capitalism, of imperialism, does not change," but its strength has declined, and this decline may deter the imperialist powers from war.[2] Now it is precisely the same concept of the unchanging essence of imperialism which the Chinese uphold—and they, too, profess that they "need peace and peaceful co-existence and have confidence in peace"; they also concede "the possibility of averting war."[3] But, in the Chinese view, this possibility can never be the result of a "sincere desire for peace" on the part of the imperialists—it can only be realized in the "peoples' struggle and class struggle" against imperialism on a broad international front. The difference is a tactical one: the Chinese evince less faith in the value of international diplomacy, negotiations, and compromises, and more faith in the increasingly militant movements in the "underdeveloped countries" and in the internal (economic) difficulties in the ad-

[2] See, for example, Khrushchev's speech to the Rumanian Party Congress, in *The Current Digest of the Soviet Press*, Vol. XII, No. 25, July 20, 1960.
[3] *New York Times*, June 24, 1960.

vanced countries of the West. However, the tactical difference implies a different evaluation of the West's reaction to its own situation. No wild risk seems to be involved in the assumption that Khrushchev believes as little in the "sincere desire for peace" on the part of the West as the Chinese do, and that the Chinese are convinced at least as much as Khrushchev that imperialist power has greatly declined (the frequent references to Mao's "paper tiger" are characteristic in this respect). But it is just this decline in strength which, to the Chinese, leads to a hardening of imperialist policy, to a desperate show of strength which vitiates the prospects of diplomatic compromises. In this phase, a soft communist diplomacy would readily appear to the West as a sign of weakness and would serve to encourage aggression. "Peaceful coexistence" thus may require a spectacular show of strength in order to deter from war—a conception that is not altogether alien to Western policy makers. The Soviet leadership (in itself divided in its evaluation of the effectiveness of soft diplomacy) viewed the U-2 incident not as isolated event but as part of a shift toward a harder policy in the West, demonstrated by the stepped-up rearmament of West Germany, the "Paris–Berlin axis," the speeches of Herter and Dillon prior to the Summit conference, etc. It may therefore be reasonable to assume that the Soviet refusal in Paris was neither emotional outburst nor abandonment of the established policy of peaceful co-existence but rather adaptation to a new, and passing, phase of international development.

A passing phase—there is no evidence that Soviet Marxism has given up its insistence on the increasing difficulties of contemporary capitalism. To be sure, their evaluation is becoming more realistic, flexible; the

eadiness to declare certain formerly tabooed con-
epts of Marxism–Leninism as historically obsolete
xtends to the very core of the doctrine.[4] There are
eports that the practicing economists question un-
esitatingly the labor theory of value; moreover, the
oncept of the progressive impoverishment of the
working classes in the capitalist countries is all but
iscarded. The 1959 edition of the textbook *Osnovy
Markzisma–Leninisma* emphasizes that the deteriora-
on of the conditions of these classes in present-day
apitalism is only a very uneven tendency, with devia-
ons and counter-tendencies, and adds:[5]

> Only slanderers and falsifiers can maintain that, accord-
> ng to the theory of Marx and Lenin, the standard of
> ving of the workers in all capitalist countries must now
> e lower than it was, for example, at the beginning of
> he twentieth century.

However, the main features of the Marxian concept of
apitalism are rigidly sustained, i.e., the theory of the
nsoluble internal contradictions of the capitalist mode
f production, and their explosive operation in the
ontemporary phase. Thus, Khrushchev's report to
he XXI Congress of the Soviet Communist Party
peaks of a new "aggravation of the general crisis of
apitalism" and states that the level of production in
he United States has "reached the ceiling which the
apitalist economy can attain"; the economic limits
f capitalism are ever more reduced by the rapid
disintegration of the colonial system." I have tried to
how (Chapter 2) that, according to Soviet Marxism,
he most promising way of utilizing the capitalist crisis

---

[4] Conversely, notions that may have appeared as embarrassing
n terms of the objectives of the Stalinist era have been re-
mphasized—for example, the "negation of the negation." For
he relative unimportance of such shifts see p. 122.
[5] Moscow 1959, p. 247.

is to undermine the ground of the "defense economy
on which the relative stability of capitalism still rests
For this reason, I continue to maintain that the USSI
has a vital interest in radical disarmament, that th
insistence on disarmament is more than "propaganda,
but that it is obviously qualified enough by fear o
aggression. With this qualification, basic Soviet polic
remains directed to the goal of defeating capitalisn
with the weapon of economic and social achievements
Khrushchev's report to the XXI Congress reaffirm
stronger than before that the USSR is moving towar
the "second phase" of communism where gradual re
duction of the working day, "polytechnical education,
and production toward the satisfaction of needs fo
all members of society become realistic policy goals
At the same time, the warnings against "leftist re
visionists" continue, and there is no doubt that scarcit
is still prevalent enough to justify regimentation an
inequality. The construction of communist societ
must proceed in stages of an objective developmen

Here, Soviet Marxism is again confronted with th
Chinese conception of communist development. Th
latter, the "simultaneous development" of industr
and agriculture, heavy and light industry, with th
establishment of large-scale rural and urban "com
munes," may well be considered as a dangerous ex
periment in "leaping" historical stages (see pp. 28 f
below). The problem of the possibility of skippin
historical stages, far from being merely a question o
Marxist orthodoxy, is a highly practical and acut
problem, presented by the factual and long-rang
co-existence of advanced capitalist and backward bu
advancing socialist countries. This "anomaly" throw
the socialist countries back on their own resources an
imposes on them the need for accelerated socialis

construction; at the same time, such acceleration proceeds on a very weak technical and material base and is susceptible to serious setbacks and disruptions, which might offer a wedge for capitalist attempts to destroy the solidarity of the communist bloc. Soviet criticism of the communes shows that the Soviet leadership is apprehensive of this possibility in the case of China; up to now, the West, by its China policy, has done much to alleviate such apprehension.

It remains to clarify a point that has caused much misunderstanding, due, in fact, to my inadequate treatment. The book recurrently stresses certain tendencies that make for assimilation, and perhaps even convergence of Western and Soviet society. In the third chapter, the "trend toward assimilation" is derived from the common features (primarily technological) of late industrial civilization. Moreover, it is stated that nationalization, "by itself," does not "constitute an essential distinction" between the two social systems "as long as production is centralized and controlled over and above the population" (p. 66). This would imply that the common technical base (the machine process as ensemble of institutions, functions, attitudes) would assert itself even through such fundamentally different economies as nationalized and private enterprise. And if one attributes such a determining role to the technical base, one might easily be induced to see in the contemporary conflict between capitalism and communism the conflict between two forms or modes of one and the same complex industrial society. I should like to dissociate myself from this position, while maintaining my emphasis on the all-embracing political character of the machine process in advanced industrial society. It is precisely this "total" character of the machine process which *limits* the tendencies toward assimilation and convergence between Western and Soviet society (in terms of time as well as structure) and generates very different potentialities of development.

At the advanced stage of industrialization, i.e., when automation is being extended to the basic industries of mass production and distribution, the technology and technics applied in the economic process are more than ever before instruments of social and political control. The satisfaction of needs (material and intellectual) takes place through scientific organization of work, scientific management, and the scientific imposition of attitudes and behavior patterns which operate beyond and outside the work process and precondition the individuals in accord with the dominant social interests. In advanced industrial society, this preconditioning is (a) in a strict sense rational, that is to say, it appears as the very manifestation of technological necessity and efficiency, and (b) it is accompanied by increasing comforts, a rising standard of living for an increasing part of the population. And to the degree that technical progress yields these tangible benefits, society can rely on the power of the economic apparatus and keep more violent means for the enforcement of compliance normally in the background. Up to this point, the two systems share the rationality of technical progress, the Soviet Union gradually "catching up" with the West in the capacity to substitute economic and ideological for military and police force. But the Soviet Union has been sharing the same trend, and has implemented it, through basically different social institutions, which are designed to make for a different development. Not the fact of nationalization or the fact of planning are decisive for this difference, but the goals imposed upon the planners by the international situation of Soviet society. The co-existence of advanced capitalism and advancing socialism involves a competition between the two systems not only in terms of efficiency and internal growth and cohesion, but also in terms of their ability to consummate technical progress. Consummation of technical progress implies automation of material production, and elimination of the wasteful, destructive, and parasitarian jobs, goods, and services maintained by obsolescent systems of domination. At this point, progress would reverse the ratio of free time and working time, in other words, the time and energy to be spent in necessary but not self-chosen activities and relaxations would be reduced to marginal time, while the bulk of the available time and energy would be the individual's own. A brief reflection will show that such development would turn quantitative (technical) progress into a qualitative change of material and intellectual culture, i.e., into a society qualitatively different from present Soviet as well as Western society.

Technical progress becomes incompatible with the two co-existent societies if and when unemployment (in traditional terms) rather than full employment appears as the measure of social wealth and freedom. Since this optimum state depends on society's ability to satisfy the vital material and intellectual needs of all its members with a minimum of imposed labor, it requires planning and control of the economy *with a view to this end;* it also requires re-education with a view to exchangeability of functions, and a trans-valuation of values, subverting a repressive work morality. To be sure, in the given conditions of the East and the West, and especially in the state of a world in which misery, starvation, and scarcity are still the lot of the vast majority of the population, such speculations are easily discarded as irresponsible or "eschatalogical." I submit again that there might be historical situations when the so-called eschatalogical view illuminates not only the realistic possibilities of the given stage, but also the extent to which this stage delays, distorts, and arrests their realization. In eschatological terms, Soviet society contains a qualitatively different society.

A considerable part of this book is devoted to showing the fundamental ambivalence in Soviet developments: the means for liberation and humanization operate for preserving domination and submission, and the theory that destroyed all ideology is used for the establishment of a new ideology. For example, polytechnical education, the very prerequisite for a future exchangeability of functions which would abolish man's lifelong enchainment by one specialized job, is accompanied by a reduction in humanistic education, and centralized planning for the satisfaction of needs includes planning for the retention of government above and against the individuals. With this fundamental ambivalence, Soviet society pays tribute to the dialectic that it sets up as an inexorable Law of History. It is perfectly true that a free society presupposes the existence of the material base of all freedom; it is also perfectly true that the creation of this base, in a still backward society in fateful competition with advanced capitalism, presupposes rigid discipline, toil, and renunciation, and the diversion of a large part of the national product to military purposes. But it is no less true that the means prejudice the end and that the dialectical circle must be broken if the new society is to emerge. This break would occur if competitive technical progress would enforce a change in the direction of technical progress, and the very backwardness from which the construction of Soviet society started may make for such a change. While the need for catching up and overtaking advanced capitalism requires planned production for the satisfaction—and increasing satisfaction—of the vital needs of the population, it militates against the planned production of wasteful and destructive goods and services and thus against the planned perpetuation and even augmentation of labor. The nationalized economy offers no internal resistance to a rationalization of technical progress which would accelerate the reduction of the working day in the realm of necessary labor, and it does not depend on the creation of new necessary labor—necessary for the continual functioning of the economic apparatus, but unnecessary for, and even at the expense of, the free development of individual faculties. An implementation of technical progress in which technology is not fused with waste and, most important, with the perpetuation of alienated labor beyond the *technical* minimum, would entail an essentially different preconditioning of the people: the values of domination and efficiency, and the lifelong work-ethics would lose their vital role in the mental household. And this speculative prospect suggests an even more unrealistic speculation: that of a "meeting between East and West" quite different from the one that is now taking place. If there is any sense in the distinction between the Oriental civilization of China and India on the one side, and Western civilization on the other, it is perhaps in the former's arrest, limitation, or methodical negation of technological rationality and, with it, of the glorification of efficiency and work. Evidently, the industrialization of the countries of Asia overrides this tradition as incompatible with the new stage of civilization, nor is it likely that the pretechnological rationality will be allowed to counteract industrialization in the long run. However, it may still find entirely new ground for reactivation on the basis of the *achievements* of industrialization: then, it may militate against the further use of technology for perpetuating individually unnecessary labor; then too, pretechnological rationality would itself become technological—perfection of technical progress toward the inner end of all technology, namely, the elimination of scarcity and toil.

The wholly unrealistic character of these prospects derives from one single fact: they are contingent on the international constellation, that is to say, on the attainment of a peaceful contest between communism and capitalism. But this contingency defines and distorts all possibilities in the contemporary period and perverts all critical analysis into utopian speculation. Thus it is more than contingency—not one unknown variable among many, but the very structure of our world. It is a world that accepts and justifies the daily risk of nuclear war as an integral part of the normal state of affairs. And such a world cannot provide the standards for what is realistic and what is not. If the prevailing state of affairs is neither normal nor necessary, it has historical alternatives that its presence and prevalence deny. Critical analysis has the task of keeping these alternatives in mind, no matter how utopian they may appear in the *status quo*.

HERBERT MARCUSE

Brandeis University
October 1960

ACKNOWLEDGMENTS

THE FIRST PART of this work is the result of my studies as a Senior Fellow at the Russian Institute, Columbia University, during the years 1952-53. The second part was prepared at the Russian Research Center, Harvard University, in 1954-55, under a special grant from the Rockefeller Foundation. I am much indebted to the Russian Research Center, and especially to its Director, William L. Langer, and Associate Director, Marshall D. Shulman, for their kindness in relinquishing to Columbia University Press their publication rights to the second part.

I also wish to express my thanks to George L. Kline, Columbia University, who prepared some of the material used in the second part of this essay; to Alfred E. Senn, for his assistance with Russian references; and to Arkadii R. L. Gurland, who offered valuable help and comments.

My friend, Barrington Moore, Jr., read the manuscript and helped me as usual with his incisive criticism.

The index was prepared by Maud Hazeltine.

HERBERT MARCUSE

Brandeis University
June, 1957

CONTENTS

PART · I

Political Tenets

1

THE MARXIAN CONCEPT
OF THE TRANSITION
TO SOCIALISM

The Original Conception

The dialectic-historical structure of Marxian theory implies that its concepts change with a change in the basic class relationships at which they aim—however, in such a way that the new content is obtained by unfolding the elements inherent in the original concept, thus preserving the theoretical consistency and even the identity of the concept. This also pertains to the notion in which the Marxian theory of the transition to socialism culminates—the notion of the objective historical coincidence between progress of civilization and the revolutionary action of the industrial proletariat. The latter is, in Marxian theory, the only social force that can accomplish the transition to a higher stage of civilization. Marx derives this coincidence from the intrinsic laws of capitalist development and thus gives it a definite place in the historical process, that is to say, the coincidence itself "passes." According to Marx, there is only one form of its passing: the proletarian revolution abolishes, with the liquidation of all classes, the proletariat as a class and thereby creates a new agent of progress—the community of free men who organize their society in accordance with the possibilities of a humane existence for all its members. But the actual development of capitalism suggested still another way of surpassing the historical coincidence, namely, through a fundamental change in the relations between the two conflicting classes whereby the proletariat fails to act as the revolutionary class. The emergence of this alternative is perhaps the most decisive factor in the development of Soviet Marxism.

The failure of the proletariat to act as the revolutionary class and the defeat of a proletarian revolution are anticipated in Marxian theory; per se, they do not constitute events which must refute the theory. In Marxian theory, they are generally explained by objective and subjective "immaturity" and considered as a temporary regression, after which the revolutionary trend will be resumed with a subsequent growth in the class consciousness of the organized proletariat. But the situation is quite different if, with or without a defeated revolution, the development of mature capitalism shows a long-range trend toward class collaboration rather than class struggle, toward national and international division rather than solidarity of the proletariat in the advanced industrial countries. In Marxian theory, capital and (wage) labor define each other, or, more specifically, the growth of the revolutionary proletariat in the long run *defines* the irreversible direction of capitalist development. Consequently, if the trend is reversed on the side of the proletariat, the capitalist development reaches a new stage to which the traditional Marxian categories no longer apply. A new historical period begins, characterized by a change in the basic class relations. Then, Marxism is faced with the task of redefining the conception of the transition to socialism and of the strategy in this period.

How did the Marxian dialectic comprehend the relation between two qualitatively different stages of the historical process—in this case, between capitalism and socialism? According to Marx, the new stage of the historical process is the "determinate negation" of the preceding stage—that is, the new stage is determined by the social structure which prevailed at the preceding stage. For example, the transition from capitalism to socialism is preconditioned by the following features of capitalist society:

(1) A high level of technological and industrial productivity which is not used to capacity for creating a humane life for all, because such use would conflict with the interest in profitable private utilization

(2) The growth of productivity beyond the limits of private control, which expresses itself in certain changes in the social institutions of capitalist enterprise (concentration of economic power coalescing with political power, decline of free competition and of the managerial function of the individual entrepreneur) and the consequent trend toward public control and appropriation

(3) The growth of the political organization of the laboring classes, who, acting as a class-conscious force, pursue their "real interest," not in, but *against* the capitalist system

These quantitative changes gain momentum until, in the proletarian revolution, they explode the prevailing structure and replace it by a qualitatively different one. Thus, the new historical level is not reached in just one leap; the transition rather consists of various phases and completes itself only through these phases. The leap matures in the highest phase of the attained stage, but the first phase of the new stage still retains the birthmarks of its origin in the preceding stage. Marx's distinction of two "phases" of socialism in the *Critique of the Gotha Program* (1875), far from being an incidental correction, follows from the very principle of the dialectical method. In their historical continuity, capitalism and socialism are joined by far stronger links than those necessitated by a period of "adjustment." During the first phase of socialism, the specific socialist principle of the free development and satisfaction of individual needs remains subordinated to the new development of the productive forces, especially of the productivity of labor. The societal wealth (material and intellectual) must be abundant enough to make possible a distribution of the social product according to individual needs regardless of the individual contribution to socially necessary labor. In economic-technological terms, this means "rationalization"; for the laborer, it means continued toil and continued delay in the free satisfaction of individual needs. The first phase of socialism still chains the worker to his specialized function, still preserves the "enslaving subordination of individuals under the division of labor," [1] and thereby the antagonism between rationality and freedom; the rational way of developing *society* conflicts with the self-realization of the *individual*. The interest of the whole still demands the sacrifice of freedom, and justice for all still involves injustice. This antagonism dissolves into the establishment of a genuine *res publica* only to the

[1] Marx, "Critique of the Gotha Program," in Marx and Engels, *Selected Works* (2 vols.; Moscow, Foreign Languages Publishing House, 1949-50), II, 23.

degree to which the socialized production creates the material and intellectual prerequisites of free and universal satisfaction of needs.

The fact that progress prior to the socialist revolution has occurred within the framework of class society and that material and intellectual productivity has been arrested by the interest of private appropriation causes in any case a time lag between the means and the end of liberation. The higher the level of material and intellectual productivity attained at the presocialist stage, the shorter the time lag, the briefer the first phase. Marx and Engels did not speculate on its duration, nor was such speculation relevant to them, for their conception of socialism implied that the qualitative change from capitalism to socialism, the "negation of the negation," takes place with the beginning of the *first* phase itself as the change from domination to self-determination. No matter how long the first phase would last, and no matter how much repression it would involve, this repression would be self-imposed by the "immediate producers," by the proletariat constituted as a state. The social distribution of labor time among the various branches of production, and thus the satisfaction of the individual needs and faculties, would be determined by collective decision of the producers of the societal wealth. Whatever coercion would have to be applied would be applied by the coerced themselves. There would be no coercive state organs separate from and above the associated laborers, for they *are* the socialist state. Wherever Marx and Engels contrast the socialist state with its preceding forms, they do so in terms of the actual *subjects* who *constitute* the state, not in terms of specific institutions. The socialist state is nothing but the "revolu-

tionary dictatorship of the proletariat";[2] socialist society is an "association of free men";[3] the productive
forces are "in the hands of producers working in
association";[4] production is organized on the basis of
"a free and equal association of the producers." [5]

The qualitative change that, in the Marxian conception, characterizes the entire first phase presupposes
the activity of a class-conscious proletariat. The proletariat that is to constitute itself as the socialist state
has been, up to the very moment of the revolution, the
object of capitalist domination and, as such, part of
the capitalist system. If this system has entered the
period of the "final crisis," if destruction and impoverishment are prevalent, then, in the Marxian expectation, the proletariat will organize itself as the
revolutionary class, follow its objective historical mission, and function within the capitalist system only as
its "gravedigger." But if capitalism continues as a
"going concern," even increasing the standard of living
of its working classes, they may become part of the
capitalist system in quite a different, positive sense.
As early as 1858 Engels noted the *Verbürgerlichung*
of the proletariat in England,[6] and in 1884 he formulated the consequence: As long as the proletariat is
not yet ripe for its self-liberation, so long will the
majority of the proletariat see in the established social

[2] *Ibid.*, p. 577.
[3] Marx, *Capital*, I, Chap. I, Sect. 4.
[4] Engels, "Anti-Dühring," in *A Handbook of Marxism*, ed. by
E. Burns (New York, International Publishers, 1935), p. 294.
[5] Engels, *Origin of the Family, Private Property, and the
State* (New York, International Publishers, 1942), p. 158. The
problem of the "withering away" of the state will be discussed
below, pp. 102 f.
[6] Letter to Marx, October 7, 1858, in Marx and Engels, *Correspondence, 1846-1895; A Selection with Commentary and
Notes* (New York, International Publishers, 1935), pp. 115-16;
see also his letter to Kautsky, September 12, 1882, in *ibid.*, pp.
399-400.

order the only possible one and will constitute politically the "tail of the capitalist class, its extreme left wing." [7] Only a virtually constant crisis could keep the class struggle acute and the proletariat class-conscious against the capitalist system, as its "absolute negation." Under such conditions, the proletariat would fulfill its "historical mission," that is, the abolition of the capitalist system. But in periods of stability and prosperity the proletariat itself is bound to come under the sway of "capitalist ideas," and its immediate (economic) interests supersede its real (historical) interest. This relation can be reversed only in the class struggle itself, that is to say, if the proletariat becomes again a *political* force and as such operates as a catalyst in the capitalist economy.

The Marxian distinction between real and immediate interest is of the greatest importance for understanding the relationship between theory and practice, between strategy and tactics in Marxism. The distinction implies a historical conflict between theory and practice, the origin and solution of which lie in the development of capitalism. The conflict thus appears as an *objective* factor. If the societal relationships determine consciousness, they do so also with respect to the proletariat. And if the societal relationships are class relationships, they also introduce the discrepancy between the form in which reality *appears* to men and the "essence" of reality. The discrepancy between essence and phenomena is a cornerstone of the Marxian method, but the metaphysical categories have become sociological ones. In the analysis of capitalism

[7] *Origin of the Family*, p. 158. For the later reinterpretation of this idea in the Leninist doctrine of the growing "labor aristocracy," see below, pp. 41 f. See E. R. Carr, *The Bolshevik Revolution, 1917-1923* (3 vols.; London, Macmillan, 1953), III, 182.

Marx describes the discrepancy in terms of the "vei
of commodity production" (reification); he derives i
from the separation of physical from intellectual worl
and from the "enslavement of man by the means o
his labor." As applied to the proletariat, although it i
"in reality" the negation of the capitalist system, thi
objective reality will not immediately appear in the
proletarian consciousness—the "class in itself" is no
necessarily "class for itself." Since, to Marx, the "es
sence" of the proletariat is a historical force whicl
the theoretical analysis only defines and demonstrates
the "real interest" of the proletariat as defined by thi
analysis is not an abstract and arbitrary construct bu
a theoretical expression of what the proletariat itsel
is—although it may not or not yet be conscious o
what it really is.

In point of fact, when Marx wrote, his concepts di
not correspond to those of the proletariat and were
probably less like them than they would be today
Marxian theory and its political goals were alien to
the existence and interest of the contemporary pro
letariat, at least to its majority. Marx and Engels were
fully aware of the gulf between essence and phenom
ena and correspondingly between theory and practice
They considered it as expressive of the historical "im
maturity" of the proletariat and believed that it would
be overcome by the ultimate political radicalization
of the working classes—itself the concomitant of the
aggravating contradictions of capitalism. Indeed, there
seemed to be a demonstrable link between the real
and the immediate interest of the proletariat in spite
of the obvious discrepancy, namely, the dehumaniza
tion and impoverishment of the laborer, which ap
peared as an objective barrier against the "sway o

capitalist ideas," against the dissolution of the revolutionary class.

To Marx and Engels, precisely because the transition from capitalism to socialism was the historical function of the proletariat as a revolutionary class, the specific political *forms* of this transition appeared as variables which could not be fixed and established by theory. Once the proletariat had constituted itself as a revolutionary class, conscious of its mission and ready to carry it out, the ways and means for accomplishing its task were to be derived from the then prevailing political and economic situation. Violence was at least not inherent in the action of the proletariat; class consciousness neither necessarily depended upon nor expressed itself in open civil warfare; violence belonged neither to the objective nor to the subjective conditions of the revolution (although it was Marx's and Engels's conviction that the ruling classes could and would not dispense with violence). It was thus more than "politics" when Marx and Engels drew attention to the possibilities of a legal and democratic transition to socialism[8]—especially at a time when the numerical and political strength of labor was growing continuously and when the labor parties were professing strongly revolutionary aims.

But while the concrete forms of the transition were

[8] We refer to the following statements: Marx's speech at Amsterdam, 1872, quoted in Iu. M. Steklov, *History of the First International* (New York, International Publishers, 1928), p. 240; Marx, "Konspekt der Debatten über das Sozialistengesetz" (written in 1878), in Marx and Engels, *Briefe an A. Bebel, W. Liebknecht, K. Kautsky, und Andere* (Moscow, Verlagsgenossenschaft Ausländischer Arbeiter in der USSR, 1933), p. 516; Engels, "Introduction to Marx's *Class Struggles in France*," in Marx and Engels, *Selected Works*, I, 109-27; Engels, *Critique of the Social Democratic Draft Program*, 1891, Sect. II.

variable, its class basis was not. The revolution was t
be the direct organized action of the *proletariat as
class*—or it was not at all. Marx and Engels did no
recognize any other agent of the revolution nor an
"substitute" for it, for substitution would signify th
immaturity of the class as such.[9] The "greatest pro
ductive force is the revolutionary class itself."[1] Th
"conquest of political power" can only be the resu
of the political movement of the working class whic
as a class opposes the ruling classes.[2] The class o
ganizes itself into a "party," but this party develop
naturwüchsig out of the "soil of modern society i
self";[3] it is the *self-organization* of the proletariat.

The Marxian conception thus maintains the identit
of the historical agent prior to and after the revolution
and the political instruments of the class struggle
especially the proletarian party, remain expressive o
this identity. The conception recognizes change
within the proletariat, in the degree of class con
sciousness, in the size and weight of the "labor aris
tocracy," etc., but these changes do not destroy th

[9] The Marxian notion of socialism implies some form o
"representation," because the proletariat cannot act *as a clas*
without organization and division of functions. However, Mar
and Engels considered only representation which was con
stituted by the class itself, that is to say, directly delegated b
and directly responsible to the "immediate producers." If th
"consciousness" of the class was "immature" or corrupted, th
leadership representing the class could help it mature, bu
could never lead it into action. In such circumstances, th
leadership would be, in a strict sense, a *theoretical* one.

[1] Marx, *The Poverty of Philosophy* (New York, Internationa
Publishers), p. 146.

[2] Marx, Letter to F. Bolte, November 23, 1871, in Marx an
Engels, *Selected Works*, II, 423; and in *Briefe und Auszüge au
Briefen von Joh. Phil. Becker, Jos. Dietzgen, Friedrich Engel
Karl Marx u. A. an F. A. Sorge und Andere*, ed. by F. A. Sorg
(Stuttgart, Dietz, 1906), p. 42.

[3] Marx, Letter to Freiligrath, in F. Mehring, *Freiligrath un
Marx in ihrem Briefwechsel* (Ergänzungshefte zur Neuen Zei
No. 12; Stuttgart, Dietz, 1912), p. 43.

identity of the class as the sole carrier of the revolution. If this class does not exist, that is, act as a class, then the socialist revolution does not exist.

Subsequent Modifications

Marx derived the afore-mentioned conclusions from a "theoretical model" of capitalism which omits all features (such as foreign trade, government intervention, "third persons") that do not pertain to the basic economic process which constitutes the capitalist system. As the analysis proceeds, in the second and third volumes of *Capital*, these omitted features are reintroduced and theory makes its way from the essence to the concrete historical reality of capitalism; the theoretical model is recast in its essential relation to the historical reality. Now, according to Marx, in its historical reality capitalism develops "countertrends" against its inherent contradictions, for example, capital export (economic and political), monopolies, government intervention. Moreover, one sector of capitalist society which had found little attention in Marx's theoretical analysis proved of decisive significance in reality, namely, the large class of peasants. The countertrends and the "neglected factor" became the focal points in the development of post-Marxian theory.

The discussion of "countertrends" moves into the center of Marxian theory with the doctrines of "finance capital" and "imperialism." These doctrines, comprising a variety of interpretations from the "revisionist" to the "orthodox" Leninist version, attempted to bring Marxist theory into line with the continued vitality of the established society and especially with the rising standard of living for the working classes in the advanced industrial countries—facts which seemed strikingly to contradict the Marxian notion of the impend-

ing final crisis of capitalism and of the impoverishment of the proletariat. In spite of the wide differences
in interpretation, the doctrines of imperialism agreed
that, around the turn of the century, capitalism had entered a new stage. The main features of the stage were
said to be the transformation of free into regimented
competition, dominated by national and international
cartels, trusts, and monopolies, the amalgamation between banking and industrial capital, government and
business, and an expansionist economic policy toward
"noncapitalist" and weaker capitalist areas (e.g., intensified exploitation of colonial and dependent countries). However, in the evaluation of this development,
the theories of imperialism were irreconcilably divided
into the "reformist" and "orthodox" camp. The theory
of the former, emerging in Eduard Bernstein's writings
of 1900-1901[4] and culminating in the doctrine of economic democracy (*Wirtschaftsdemokratie*),[5] maintained that, within the framework of "organized
capitalism," the proletariat could continue to improve
its economic as well as its political position and ultimately establish socialism by legal and democratic
means through the increasing economic and political
influence of organized labor. In sharp contrast, the
orthodox interpretation, in its extreme represented by
Lenin, saw in the growth of capitalism a tenuous and
temporary stabilization bound to explode in armed
conflicts among the imperialist powers and in sharpening economic crises. Lenin explained the reformist
tendencies among the proletariat in terms of the rise

[4] See Eduard Bernstein, *Evolutionary Socialism: A Criticism
and Affirmation*, trans. by Edith C. Harvey (New York,
Huebsch, 1909).
[5] Formulated by Rudolf Hilferding at the conference of the
German Social Democratic Party at Kiel, 1927, and in Fritz
Naphtali, *Wirtschaftsdemokratie*, published by the German
Trade Union Federation, Berlin, 1928.

of a small "labor aristocracy," "corrupted" by high wages paid out of monopolistic surplus profits, with a vested interest in the established system.

We are here concerned only with the Leninist interpretation. The emergence of Leninism as a new form of Marxism is determined by two main factors: (1) the attempt to draw the peasantry into the orbit of Marxian theory and strategy, and (2) the attempt to redefine the prospects of capitalist and revolutionary development in the imperialist era. The two main currents of Leninist thought are closely interrelated; the viability of advanced capitalism (unexpected from the traditional Marxist point of view) and, consequently, the continued strength of reformism among the proletariat in the advanced capitalist countries called almost inevitably for a shift in Marxist emphasis to the backward countries, which were predominantly agricultural and where the weakness of the capitalist sector seemed to offer better chances for a revolution. True, the notion that the capitalist chain must be broken at its "weakest link"—a notion stressed by Stalin after the revolution—was originally Trotsky's rather than Lenin's, but the whole trend of Leninist thought from the beginning is in this direction. When the "workers' and peasants' revolution," rather than the workers' revolution, becomes the center of Soviet Marxism, it is not only because the revolution happened to be successful in Russia but because the revolutionary potential of the industrial working class seemed to recede throughout the advanced capitalist world. It was this fact that, in the long run, decided the development of Soviet Marxism. We therefore take as a starting point Lenin's analysis of the situation of the proletariat at the imperialist stage.

Significant in this interpretation is the underestima-

tion of the economic and political potentialities of
capitalism, and of the change in the position of the
proletariat. In fact, the refusal to draw the theoretical
consequences from the new situation characterizes the
entire development of Leninism and is one of the chief
reasons for the gap between theory and practice in
Soviet Marxism. For, while Lenin from the beginning
of his activity reoriented the revolutionary strategy
of his party in accordance with the new situation, his
theoretical conception did not follow suit. Lenin's retention of the classical notion of the revolutionary
proletariat, sustained with the help of the theory of
the labor aristocracy and the avant garde, revealed its
inadequacy from the beginning. Even prior to the
First World War it became clear that the "collabora-
tionist" part of the proletariat was quantitatively and
qualitatively different from a small upper stratum that
had been corrupted by monopoly capital, and that the
Social Democratic Party and trade union bureaucracy
were more than "traitors"—rather that their policy
reflected pretty exactly the economic and social condition of the majority of the organized working classes
in the advanced industrial countries. And indeed,
Lenin's strategy of the revolutionary avant garde
pointed to a conception of the proletariat which went
far beyond a mere reformulation of the classical Marxian concept; his struggle against "economism" and
the doctrine of spontaneous mass action, his dictum
that class consciousness has to be brought upon the
proletariat "from without" anticipate the later factual
transformation of the proletariat from the subject to
an object of the revolutionary process. True, Lenin's
What Is to Be Done? [6] where these ideas found their

---

[6] Lenin, *Chto delat'?* (What Is to Be Done?) appeared first
in 1902.

classical formulation, was written for the struggle of
the Russian Marxists for leadership over a backward
proletariat, but their implications go far beyond this
context. The ultimate target is stated at the beginning
of Lenin's pamphlet: it is the rising reformist camp
in "international social democracy," represented for
Lenin by Bernstein and Millerand, who demanded a
"decided change from revolutionary social democracy
to bourgeois reformism." Moreover, the phrase "class
consciousness from without" did not originate from the
Russian situation but was coined by Karl Kautsky in
his polemics against the draft of the new program of
the Austrian Social Democratic Party.[7] Lenin aimed
beyond the exigencies of the specific Russian situation,
at a general international development in Marxism,
which in turn reflected the trend of large sections of
organized labor toward "class cooperation." As this
trend increased, it threatened to vitiate the notion of
the proletariat as the revolutionary subject on which
the whole Marxist strategy depended. Lenin's formulations intended to save Marxian orthodoxy from the
reformist onslaught, but they soon became part of a
conception that no longer assumed the historical coincidence between the proletariat and progress which
the notion of the "labor aristocracy" still retained. The
groundwork was laid for the development of the Leninist party where the true interest and the true consciousness of the proletariat were lodged in a group
different from the majority of the proletariat. The
centralistic organization, which was first justified by
and applied to the "immaturity" of backward conditions, was to become the general principle of strategy
on an international scale.

[7] See *What Is to Be Done?* (New York, International Publishers, 1929), p. 40.

The construction of the Leninist party (or par
leadership) as the real representative of the proletari:
could not bridge the gap betewen the new strateg
and the old theoretical conception. Lenin's strateg
of the avant garde acknowledged in fact what
denied in theory, namely, that a fundamental chang
had occurred in the objective and subjective cond
tions for the revolution.

In his *Finanzkapital*,[8] published in 1910, Rudo
Hilferding interpreted this change in terms of Marxia
theory. He pointed out that, under the leadership (
finance capital, the entire national economy would b
mobilized for expansion, and that this expansior
through the collusion of giant monopolistic and sem
monopolistic enterprises, would tend toward large
scale international integration, economic as well a
political. On this new intercontinental market, produc
tion and distribution would be to a great extent cor
trolled and regimented by a cartel of the mos
powerful capitalist interests. In the huge dominio
of such a "general cartel," the contradictions of th
capitalist system could be greatly controlled, profit
for the ruling groups secured, and a high level c
wages for labor within the dominion sustained—:
the expense of the intensified exploitation of market
and populations outside the dominion. Hilferdin
thought that such international capitalist plannin
would require the abolition of democratic liberalism i
the economy as well as in the political and ideologica

---

[8] *Das Finanzkapital; Eine Studie über die jüngste Entwick
lung des Kapitalismus* (Marx-Studien III; Vienna, Wiener Volks
buchhandlung, 1910). Hilferding's term designates not merel
a specific form of capital, but a specific form of capitalist or
ganization. He identifies its two essential elements as (a) th
"abolition" (*Aufhebung*) of free competition by the formatio
of cartels and trusts, and (b) the ever closer amalgamation be
tween "banking capital" and "industrial capital."

phere; individualism and humanism would be replaced by an aggressive militarist nationalism and
authoritarianism. Similar ideas were subsequently
(1914) advanced by Karl Kautsky in his concept of
ultra-imperialism." [9]

These developments were presented only as tendencies the realization of which for any length of time
was doubted by Hilferding as well as Kautsky. Nor
did these writers draw the full conclusions concerning
the changing class situation of the proletariat. But
the economic and political conditions had been outlined under which the capitalist world could be stabilized and hierarchically integrated—conditions
which in Marxian theory appeared as utopian unless
the actual forces which would supersede the contradictions and conflicts among the imperialist powers
developed. Once they materialized, an economic basis
for integration could indeed emerge. It did emerge,
very gradually and with many regressions and breaks,
under the impact of two World Wars, atomic productivity, and the growth of Communist power. These
events altered the structure of capitalism as defined by
Marx and created the basis of a new economic and
political organization of the Western world.[1] This
basis came to be utilized effectively only after the
Second World War. From then on, the conflicting com-

[9] Kautsky, "Der Imperialismus," *Die Neue Zeit*, XXXII, 2,
No. 21 (September 11, 1914), 921.
[1] Soviet Marxism maintains—and indeed must maintain if the
Marxian conception is to be preserved—that these events are
intrinsically related: the "permanent war economy," as the
sole outlet for the imperialist contradictions, leads to atomic
productivity, and the latter enforces economic as well as political
integration of the Western powers. According to this conception, the events which bring about the transformation of the
Western world are not extraneous but rather internal to the
dynamic of the capitalist system, and the same forces that make
for war make for progress in productivity and for "temporary
stabilization."

petitive interests among the Western nations wer
gradually integrated and superseded by the funda
mental East-West conflict, and an intercontinenta
political economy took shape—in extent much smalle
than the former free world market, but susceptible t
a planned regulation of that blind "anarchy" in whic
Marxism saw the root of capitalist contradictions. A
the same time, the laboring classes were split on a
international scale into (to use Toynbee's terms) a
internal and *external* proletariat, the latter consistin
of those (urban and rural) proletarian and semipro
letarian classes, outside and inside the area of effectiv
reconstruction, which did not benefit from it by highe
wages, better living conditions, or greater politica
influence.

The external proletariat (including, as its larges
part, the peasantry), which came to provide the Sovie
leadership with a mass basis for the struggle agains
capitalism after the First World War, emerged as
historical "subject" seemingly by virtue of (from th
Marxian viewpoint) an exogenous event, namely, b
virtue of the fact that the revolution succeeded i
backward Russia, failed to materialize in the ad
vanced industrial countries, and subsequently sprea
from Russia into preindustrial areas, while the ad
vanced industrial countries continued to remain im
mune. But this event was not quite as exogenous a
it seems. The gradual "immunization" of decisive area
of Western society had already begun to show it
effectiveness prior to the First World War; the na
tionalist attitude of the Social Democratic parties i
1914—at that time the unchallenged Marxist organiza
tion of labor—was only its most conspicuous mani
festation. The immunization then proved its power i
the Central European revolutions from 1918 to 192;

here the majority of organized labor defeated the ommunist assault in alliance with the bourgeoisie id the army. In England, the predominance of the eformist Labour Party had never been seriously disirbed. In France and Italy, Communist strength connued to trail far behind that of Social Democracy; id in Germany, the only country where it came to a owerful resurgence after the defeat, Social Demoatic as well as Communist labor succumbed quickly the Fascist regime. The sustained weakness of the evolutionary potential in the advanced industrial ountries confined the revolution to that area where ie proletariat had not been thus affected and where ie regime had shown political disintegration together with economic backwardness.

Marxian theory explained the rising standard of ving, which lay at the economic roots of the imunization process, in terms of the growing producvity of labor, the effective organization of the dustrial workers, which counteracted the pressure 1 the wage level, and in terms of monopolistic surplus ofits in the most advanced capitalist areas. According to Marxism, none of these factors could neutralize r any length of time the inherent contradictions of ie capitalist mode of production. The benefits for the orking class were expected to be wiped out periodally by wars and crises since there was no basis for ng-range international capitalist consolidation. This terpretation did not provide for the possibility (soon become a fact) that such an international basis ould materialize. On it, Western industrial society eated its new economic and political institutions. he catastrophic violence, the unprecedented extent ' physical and cultural destruction, and also the jually unprecedented growth of technical produc-

tivity which characterized the period after 1918, co
responded to the scope of the task. It was the ve.
structure of the established civilization that was cha
lenged and that had to be reaffirmed against a cor
peting civilization. The technological and politic
potential developed in this struggle made it soc
appear that minor adjustments would not suffice
meet the challenge. The need for the total mobilizatic
of all material and mental forces necessitated th
abolition of laissez-faire in economic and cultur
life, the methodical control of the political proces
and national regrouping under the actual hierarchy
economic power—at the expense of cherished trac
tional sovereignties. The overriding interest of Weste
society as a whole modified national and class interest
the national parties aligned themselves with the inte
national economic and political forces. Labor was n
exception and, at the end, Social Democracy becan
part of the Western, and Communism part of th
Eastern, orbit. For Marxism, the capitalist world ha
never come closer to the dreaded specter of a "gener
cartel" which would replace the anarchy of capitali
production and distribution by ultraimperialist pla
ning. And it was the very progress of the Soviet syste
which had promoted the realization of this dreade
possibility.

___

2

SOVIET MARXISM:

THE BASIC

SELF-INTERPRETATION

The Leninist Heritage

A comparison between the above analysis of the historical presuppositions of Soviet Marxism with the official Soviet pronouncements shows that the latter do not explicitly acknowledge these presuppositions. Leninist as well as Stalinist theory has recurrently and emphatically denied the possibility of a long-range international integration of the Western world. The readjustments of the post-Stalinist period, while explicitly rejecting the "theory of absolute stagnation of capitalism" and Stalin's theses on the shrinkage of the capitalist system, still retain the notion of the "intensification of the capitalist contradictions" in the present era.[1] Soviet Marxism has equally emphatically

[1] See Mikoyan's speech, February 16, 1956, at the Twentieth Congress of the Communist Party of the Soviet Union, in *XX S"ezd Kommunisticheskoi Partii Sovetskogo Soiuza: Stenograficheskii otchet* (The Twentieth Congress of the Communist Party of the Soviet Union: Stenographic Account) (2 vols.; Moscow, Gospolitizdat, 1956), I, 319-21; Khrushchev's speech of February 14, in *ibid.*, I, 14-20; also New York *Times*, February 19, 1956; and Khrushchev's speech of November 6, 1957 (as broadcast by Moscow Home Service, p. A-47).

denied the concomitant changes in the structure o
the laboring class in the Western countries; the classi
cal Marxist notion of the revolutionary proletaria
having been a mainstay of Soviet theory. However, a
the decisive policies of constructing socialism in th
Soviet orbit are based on the structural changes whic'
characterize the contemporary period, and on th
decline of the revolutionary proletariat in the Wester.
world. This dichotomy raises the problem of the ob
jective sincerity of Soviet Marxist theoretical pro
nouncements—part of the larger problem of th
relationship between Soviet theory and practice.

We have already mentioned that "Aesopian lan
guage" is systematically employed *within* the Sovie
Marxist camp itself and for Marxist audiences an
communications. Soviet Marxism continues to use th
"orthodox" Marxian notions to designate situations an
policies which obviously contradict these notions. Un
der these circumstances it would seem to be ap
propriate to dismiss Soviet Marxism as mer
"propaganda." This is a deceptive solution, becaus
the distinction between "propaganda" and "truth
presupposes a demonstrable "truth" with whic'
propaganda can be contrasted. If it is maintaine
that the truth expresses itself only in the practice an
not in the theory of Soviet Marxism, that the theor
serves only as an ideological prop for mass manipula
tion, then this contention has to be proved. It is b
no means self-evident in the face of the difficultie
which the regime creates for itself by constantly teach
ing and publicizing Marxian ideas that can be recon
ciled with reality only by great expenditure of physica
and intellectual force. The fact is that, regardless o
its "level," the exposition of Marxist theory continue
to be one of the main efforts of the regime, and th

tension between theory and practice continues to exist.

But if it seems inappropriate to dismiss the whole of theory as propaganda, it seems equally inappropriate to retain parts of it as the truth and classify others as "subterfuge." There are no criteria for such a selection —unless we can detect certain Marxist notions that remain constant through the various changes in Soviet theory and strategy. Then it might be possible to arrive at an identification of the "basic elements," and to derive the "revisions" and "rejections" from these elements, thus obtaining a body of theoretical principles in relationship to practice. It is this approach which guides the subsequent discussion.

The formation of Soviet Marxist theory proceeds on the basis of Lenin's interpretation of Marxism, without going back to original Marxian theory. A brief summary of the essential links between Leninism and subsequent Soviet Marxism will suffice to clarify the starting point.

We suggested above that the characteristic features of emerging Leninism, i.e., the shift in the revolutionary agent from the class-conscious proletariat to the centralized party as the avant garde of the proletariat and the emphasis on the role of the peasantry as ally of the proletariat, developed under the impact of the sustained strength of capitalism at the "imperialist stage." The conception which was initially aimed at the "immaturity" of the Russian proletariat became a principle of international strategy in the face of the continued reformist attitude of the "mature" proletariat in the advanced industrial countries. To counteract the integration of a large sector of organized labor into the capitalist system, the "subjective factor" of revolutionary strategy is monopolized by the Party, which assumes the character of a professional revolutionary organization directing the proletariat.

The Leninist conception may be presented as a development of the Marxian distinction between the "immediate" and the "real" interest (and consciousness) of the proletariat. Here are the principal stages: (*a*) Societal being determines consciousness: the individual proletarian, in capitalist relationships of production, desires to improve his individual conditions immediately and continually within the capitalist system. (*b*) The "economistic" policy of the trade unions, in achieving such improvement, sustains the proletariat as an exploited class and thereby sustains capitalist society; but at the same time it modifies the social structure in so far as it provides a basis for "class peace." (*c*) This change in the social structure "deflects" the proletariat from its objective historical position as the revolutionary class which can liberate itself only by abolishing the capitalist system. (*d*) The objective historical position can be "rescued" only by subordinating the immediate subjective interest to the real interest of the class, by transforming the economic into a political struggle. This task is the function of the Leninist party. Since, according to Marxian theory, the economic struggle by itself can never achieve more than a brief improvement, the capitalist process, through recurrent depressions and crises, will redress the balance and lead to the radicalization of the proletariat, thus reestablishing the coincidence of its immediate and real interests.

But what happens when the process (*c*) affects the bulk of the proletariat in the advanced capitalist countries? Has not Marxian theory then lost the mass basis required for its realization? And is not the connection between theory and reality also lost, unless the former redefines itself by redefining the latter? These questions seem to have driven Leninist theory toward a reevaluation of contemporary capitalist development, which has become the theoretical foundation for the doctrine of "socialism in one country."

This doctrine, which predates the Bolshevik Revolution, revealed itself from the beginning as defined and determined by the new stage of industrial society. Lenin's "law of the uneven development of capitalism" was at first only the expression of an actual state of affairs, but the inferences drawn from it form the very core of Soviet Marxism. Lenin noted that "uneven economic and political development is an absolute law of capitalism" and immediately added, therefore, "the victory of socialism is, at the beginning, possible in a few capitalist countries," or even in a single capitalist country.[2] The conclusion clearly implies here that socialism may be victorious first in a few or even in one single *advanced* capitalist country, while the more backward countries will lag behind. One year later, Lenin wrote that socialism will achieve victory first in one or several countries while the others will remain bourgeois or "pre-bourgeois" for some time.[3]

Lenin retained the Marxian conclusion that the socialist revolution will be the result of the exploding contradictions in a *fully matured* capitalist country—and not even the triumph of the Bolshevik Revolution made him abandon this conviction. His hesitation to

[2] "The United States of Europe Slogan" (written in 1915), in *The Strategy and Tactics of World Communism*, House Document No. 619, Supplement I (Washington, D.C., U.S. Government Printing Office, 1948), p. 29; Lenin, *Selected Works* (12 vols.; New York, International Publishers, 1937-38), V, 141.

[3] "Voennaia programma proletarskoi revoliutsii" (The War Program of the Proletarian Revolution), in *Sochineniia* (Works) (3d ed., 30 vols.; Moscow, Institut Lenina, 1928-37), XIX, 325. See also *History of the Communist Party of the Soviet Union* (New York, International Publishers, 1939), p. 169.

acknowledge the socialist character of the revolution
is well known—a hesitation in spite of his thesis
that the "bourgeois-democratic revolution" had to
be surpassed by a workers' and peasants' revolution
which would replace the parliamentary republic by
a Soviet republic. As late as March, 1919, he called
the October Revolution a "bourgeois revolution in
so far as the class struggle on the countryside had
not yet developed." [4] And he added that only in the
summer of 1918 did the real proletarian revolution on
the countryside begin. He clung to the notion that
the Russian Revolution must be rescued by the
German revolution.

But it is precisely Lenin's belief in the tentative
and preliminary character of the Russian Revolution
which leads him to formulations clearly foreshadow-
ing the Stalinist policy. Socialism presupposes capitalism—or at least the achievements of capitalism,
namely, a high degree of industrialization, a high
productivity of labor, and a highly developed, skilled,
and disciplined labor force. Stages in this sequence
may perhaps be "jumped" (Lenin was hesitant also
with respect to this problem[5]), but without the
achievements of a fully industrialized and rationalized
economy there can be no socialism, no distribution of
the social product according to individual needs and
faculties. In a backward country, industrialization
has priority over socialization, that is, over production
and distribution according to individual needs. At the

[4] His speech on rural policy to the Eighth Congress of the
Russian Communist Party, March 23, 1918, in *Sochineniia*
(Works), XXIV, 162.
[5] See for example the contradictory statements in "Two Tactics
of Social Democracy" (written in 1905), in *Selected Works*,
III, 75; and in the report of the Commission on the National
and Colonial Question to the Second World Congress of the
Comintern, 1920, in *Selected Works*, X, 239-44.

meeting of the All-Russian Central Executive Committee in April, 1918, in his polemic against the "left Communists" who foresaw the "road to state capitalism," Lenin declared:

> In reality, state capitalism would be a step forward for us. If we were capable of attaining state capitalism in Russia within a short time, this would be a victory. . . . I said that state capitalism would be our savior. If we would have it in Russia, then the transition to full socialism would be easy and certain. For state capitalism is a system of centralization, integration, control, and socialization. And this is precisely what we lack.[6]

And one month later he quoted a statement of September, 1917, to the effect that "state-monopolistic capitalism is the complete material preparation for socialism," the "anteroom" of socialism, the historical stage immediately preceding socialism, and he added, "Is it not clear, that, in the material, economic sense, in terms of production, we are not yet in the 'anteroom' of socialism? And that we cannot reach the door to socialism by any other way than through this 'anteroom'?"[7]

The implications of these statements remain obscured by the fact that the German revolution of 1918 seemed to unleash that chain of revolutions in mature countries which would restore the "orthodox" way of international revolution. The Soviet state would not only be "protected" by the proletarian state of a highly developed industrial country but would also share in its technical and material wealth, and the transition to socialism would thus be secured and

---

[6] *Sochineniia* (Works), XXII, 482.
[7] "O 'levom' rebiachestve i mel'koburzhuaznosti" (On "Leftist" Infantilism and Petty-Bourgeois Attitudes), *Pravda*, May 9-11, 1918.

accelerated. The almost desperate orientation toward
Germany is contained in the record of the meetings
of the Comintern and its executive committee and
of Lenin's speeches during the first years of the
revolution. But from about 1921 on, Soviet policy
drew the consequences from the defeat of the German
revolution. In view of the central role which the
relationship between mature capitalism and the transition to socialism plays in Marxian theory, the
failure of the German revolution—coupled with the
growing leadership of the United States in the reconstruction of the Western world—seemed to necessitate a reevaluation of the international development.
If the capitalist potential should, for a long time to
come, prove stronger than the revolutionary potential,
if not even the First World War and its effect on the
economy could break the hold of reformism over
the "mature proletariat," then the historical agent
of the revolution had changed not only in a geographical but also in a social sense. If there was real
"capitalist stabilization," then not only would the
Soviet state, for a long time to come, "coexist" with
the far more powerful capitalist world, but it would
also have to look toward the developing revolutionary
movement in the colonial and semicolonial countries
as more than a mere "reserve" for the revolutionary
army. Not only the international strategy, but also
the construction of socialism in Soviet society, would
have to be redefined.

Lenin's *Pravda* article, "Better Fewer, But Better,"
(March, 1923), combines the traditional and the new
evaluation of the international development in a
few telescoped propositions. They center on the statement that the Western European capitalist countries
are not accomplishing their way to socialism "in the

way we formerly expected." [8] Lenin continued: They "are not accomplishing it by the even ripening of socialism, but by the exploitation of some countries by others . . . combined with the exploitation of the whole of the East." How does imperialist exploitation of vanquished capitalist countries (in Lenin's context, Germany specifically) alter the "expected" accomplishment of socialism? Lenin's text suggests several answers: (*a*) by shifting the capitalist center from Central Europe to the West, ultimately to the United States;[9] (*b*) by rapidly drawing "the East, India, China, etc.," into the capitalist world system; (*c*) by, at the same time, accelerating nationalist and revolutionary movements in the East (and in the vanquished capitalist countries?). Lenin's propositions imply, on the one hand, capitalist growth (through the "new exploitation of the defeated countries and of the East") and, on the other, growth of the revolutionary potential "in the East" ("we have the advantage in that the whole world is now passing into a movement that must give rise to world socialist revolution").

The difficulties presented by these formulations are augmented by Lenin's statement that "we are laboring under the disadvantage that the imperialists have succeeded in splitting the world into two camps." [1] The "disadvantage" can only be explained

---

[8] In *Selected Works*, IX, 399.
[9] In 1915, in his article "The United States of Europe Slogan," Lenin wrote: "In comparison with the *United States of America*, Europe as a whole signifies economic stagnation. . . . The times when the cause of democracy and Socialism was associated with Europe alone have gone forever." *Selected Works*, V, 140-41. Italics added.
[1] *Selected Works*, IX, 399. In Stalinist theory, in view of the greatly increased strength of the Communist camp, this "split" appears as an *advantage*, and as a success, not of the "imperialists," but of the Communists.

in terms of the new strength accruing to capitalism through exploitation of the vanquished countries, "combined" with the exploitation of the whole East, and through the collaboration of the working classes of the imperialist victor countries. Lenin stressed the fact that "a number of the oldest states in the West are in a position to utilize their victory for the purpose of making a number of insignificant concessions to their oppressed classes which, insignificant as they are, nevertheless retard the revolutionary movement in these countries and create something which has the appearance of *class peace.*" [2]

This comes close to Hilferding's conception of the establishment of an effective national interest uniting labor and capital in advanced imperialist countries. However, in contrast, Lenin's analysis led to a "guidance" for Soviet policy which was based on the expectation of interimperialist *conflicts* and which has become "obligatory" for Soviet Marxism. Here again, the ambiguities of Lenin's statements are striking. He raised the question of how to "save ourselves from the impending conflict with these imperialist countries," thereby implying the typical Stalinist contraposition of the Soviet and the imperialist camp. But he immediately answered with the "hope that the internal antagonisms and conflicts between the thriving imperialist countries of the West and the thriving imperialist countries of the East will give us a second respite," [3] without discussing the obvious possibility that the former conflict (between the

[2] *Ibid.*, IX, 398. Italics added.

[3] *Ibid.*, IX, 399. The conception of the respite or "breathing space" began to play a decisive role in Soviet foreign and domestic policy in 1920. See E. H. Carr, *The Bolshevik Revolution, 1917-1923* (3 vols.; London, Macmillan, 1953), III, 318 ff.

imperialist countries and the Soviet Union) may "neutralize" or "suspend" the conflict within the imperialist camp. In any case, he declared, the "final outcome" of the struggle between socialism and imperialism, namely, the victory of socialism, is "absolutely assured" by the fact that the population of "Russia, India, China, etc.," constitutes the overwhelming majority of the earth's population, and is rapidly being "drawn into the struggle for its emancipation." What was "interesting" to Lenin was not the final outcome, but the Soviet policy of "preventing the West European counterrevolutionary states from crushing us." And he held that the Soviet policy of "ensuring our existence" until this conflict erupted, must aim at making the East "more civilized." And this in turn made it necessary "to develop electrification, hydro-peat, to construct Volkhovstroy, etc." "In this and in this alone lies our hope." [4]

Without reconciling them, Lenin's analysis contains the old and the new elements of the situation: the "internal antagonisms and conflicts within the imperialist camp" stand side by side with the "impending conflict" between this camp and the Soviet state. The policy conclusions which Lenin derived from this analysis take equal account of both sets of contradictions.

The interimperialist contradictions. The survival of the Soviet state depends ultimately on them. The Soviet state must obtain and preserve a long "respite" by utilizing the conflicts among the imperialist powers. Thus Lenin had already formulated the substance of Soviet foreign policy at the Eighth All-Russian Congress of Soviets in December, 1920: "Our exist-

[4] *Selected Works*, IX, 400-401.

ence depends, first, on the existence of a radical split
in the camp of the imperialist Powers." [5]

*The contradictions between the capitalist world
and the Soviet state.* Temporary stabilization and
"class peace" in the victorious capitalist countries
shifts the revolutionary potential from these countries
to the "revolutionary and nationalist East." The shift
is more than a geographical change—it signifies the
emergence of a new agent of the historical process.
Lenin designated this agent only as the population
of "Russia, India, China, etc." The vagueness of this
designation is characteristic: Lenin did not introduce
a new theoretical concept which would alter the
structure of Marxian doctrine, nor did he elaborate
the notion of the new international character of the
class struggle. But his policy guidance is clear: the
interimperialist contradictions are the decisive ones;
they must be utilized for the accomplishment of the
main task—Soviet industrialization.

Soviet Marxism has followed Lenin's twofold guidance: its main theoretical effort has been to correlate
the two sets of contradictions as a basis for policy,
and to determine their relative weight. We cannot
discuss here the various turns and variants of the
Soviet Marxist analysis of the international situation
from the Fifth Congress of the Comintern in 1924
to the Twentieth Party Congress in 1956, but we
shall try to demonstrate that the basic Soviet conception of capitalist development has not fundamentally changed throughout the entire period. To
be sure, the zigzag of right and left turns has continued in Communist tactics, but since the Sixth
World Congress at the latest, they appear as short-

[5] *Sochineniia* (Works), XXVI, 14-15. For translation see
Carr, *The Bolshevik Revolution*, III, 331.

lived tactical trials in contradistinction—and often in conflict—to the underlying conception and strategy. In order to clarify this distinction between tactical devices and the basic conception, we shall begin by trying to identify the Soviet Marxist categories which have remained constant throughout the various turns during the Stalinist period.

The Analysis of Contemporary Capitalism

Soviet Marxism sees the entire capitalist development since the First World War as comprising *one* period: the subdivisions of this period appear to represent only stages in the growth of one and the same basic trend. Its main features[6] as interpreted by Soviet Marxism are as follows:

1. The triumph of monopoly capitalism over the surviving elements of "free" capitalism

2. The organization of monopoly capitalism on an international scale on the basis of a permanent (potential or actual) war economy, with growing "state capitalist tendencies"

3. Economic and political subjugation of the weaker capitalist powers by the stronger, and of the stronger by the strongest capitalist power (the United States); thereby creation of large intercontinental areas of "exploitation"

4. Total mobilization of all human, material, and technical resources for the struggle against communism

[6] They are taken from: (a) the program, theses, and resolutions of the Comintern; (b) the theoretical statements of Soviet leaders that have been "canonized" as obligatory; (c) the principal discussions and papers of Soviet economists, especially the discussions of 1947 (the Varga controversy), 1949, and 1950, and the analyses of the contemporary capitalist situation in *Voprosy Ekonomiki* (Problems of Economics) after the Nineteenth Party Congress. Specific references will be given below.

5. Restriction or outright abolition of the democratic process, of civil and political liberties, and
of liberal and humanitarian ideologies

6. Containment, by force and by "corruption,"
of the revolutionary potential within the capitalist
system

7. Global sociopolitical division into the "imperialist" and "socialist" camp

Before explaining this interpretation, three questions
must be answered: (1) How does Soviet Marxism
justify the assumption of one basic trend for the
entire period after the First World War in view of
the obvious difficulty of placing fascism and the
Western democracies, the "grand alliance" and the
"cold war" on one common denominator? (2) How
is the notion of the successful containment of the
revolutionary forces within the capitalist system reconcilable with the recurrent "left turns" and aggressive ventures of Communist strategy, and (3) with
the spectacular growth of the French and Italian
Communist parties after the Second World War?

As to the first question, Soviet Marxism see fascism
as a specific phase in the national and international
class struggle, namely, as the open, terroristic "dictatorship of the most reactionary, most chauvinistic
and most imperialist elements of finance capital." [7]
This dictatorship is the attempt to "solve" the capitalist crisis by intensified exploitation of the working
classes and of the colonies, by the "enslavement of
the weak nations," and by preparing or actually

[7] Thirteenth *Plenum of the Executive Committee of the
Comintern: Theses and Decisions* (New York, Workers Library
Publishers, 1934), pp. 3 f.; Dimitrov's report to the Seventh
World Congress of the Comintern, 1935, in *United Front
Against Fascism* (New York, New Century Publishers, 1935),
pp. 5-7.

waging war against the Soviet Union. This formulation contains all the chief characteristics subsequently applied to "Anglo-American or American imperialism." Such transfer is implied in Point 3 of the Soviet Marxist analysis: the hierarchical international organization of contemporary capitalism under the supremacy of the strongest economic power, necessitating the sacrifice of traditional sovereignties and democratic liberties. The economic basis for German fascist supremacy was too narrow. This "anomaly" was corrected by the Second World War, which redressed the international balance and redivided the spheres of influence in accordance with actual economic strength, that is, with the emergence of the United States as the strongest capitalist power. Fascism and the defeat of fascism thus appear as "logical" steps in the international reorganization of monopoly capitalism.

But if the struggle against the Soviet Union is one of the essential elements of this reorganization (Point 4), how can one explain the alliance between the capitalist West and the USSR during the Second World War? Soviet Marxism has two answers: (*a*) the Western powers needed the aid of the USSR to defeat German fascism, and (*b*) even during the alliance, the Western struggle against the USSR continued (cited as examples are the delay in opening the second front, Churchill's Balkan strategy, and the Western powers' alleged efforts to obtain a separate peace with Germany).

As to the second and third questions, before the Second World War, Soviet Marxism subdivided the contemporary capitalist development into three periods. The acute revolutionary situation after the First World War (the "first period") was followed by a

period of "relative stabilization" (the "second period").
In his first Political Report to the Central Committee,
delivered at the Fourteenth Party Congress in 1925,
Stalin analyzed the international situation in terms
of a "stabilization of capitalism." He called it a temporary and "partial" stabilization,[8] and three years later,
at the Sixth World Congress of the Comintern, the
coming of a "third period" was announced. The Communist parties were directed toward leftist radicalism.
Mass demonstrations in the face of resolute armed
resistance, the disastrous struggle against "social
fascist" labor parties and trade unions, alliances with
the extreme right, the proclamation of a new "revolutionary tide" in China—these were the manifestations
of the left turn, which seemed to find its economic
justification in the great depression of 1929. In 1932,
the Twelfth Plenum of the Executive Committee of
the Comintern again announced the "end of capitalist
stabilization" and the beginning of a new cycle of
wars and revolutions. The "third period" was said
to be characterized by a "growing revolutionary
upsurge" in the capitalist countries and by a "sharpening of the economic crisis." [9] This is perhaps the
most extreme "left turn" the Comintern made after
the failure of the Central European revolution, and
in his report to the Plenum on the international
situation Kuusinen stated that every effort should be
made to "prepare the proletariat and the rest of the
working population for the struggle for power in

[8] *Political Report of the Central Committee* (Moscow, Foreign Languages Publishing House, 1950), pp. 10 f.
[9] *Capitalist Stabilization Has Ended; Thesis and Resolutions
of the Twelfth Plenum of the Executive Committee of the
Communist International* (New York, Workers Library Publishers, 1932), p. 7.

the new period." [1] But the strategy directions seem
to presuppose quite a different evaluation of the
capitalist situation. The thesis on Kuusinen's report
adopted by the Twelfth Plenum has, in contrast to
the report itself, a predominantly defensive tone.
Although retaining the phrase, "the growing revolutionary upsurge," the thesis calls for the struggle
against the "capitalist offensive" [2] rather than for the
seizure of power, for waging the class struggle "on
the basis of the united front from below," [3] for a
mass political strike when the "proper condition for
it exists," [4] and ends with the usual exhortation to the
Communist parties to direct the movement "along the
channel of the World Socialist Revolution."

Thus even the most "leftist" Comintern program
does not contradict our assumption that Stalinist
strategy implied effective containment of the revolutionary potential in the Western world after the
failure of the Central European revolutions. The
strategy of the "united front against fascism," which
followed in 1935, went one step further in acknowl-
edging the decline of the revolutionary potential in
the West, by committing the Communist parties to
a "minimum program" within the framework of the
"bourgeois-democratic" state.

The situation at the end of the Second World War
may serve as another illustration of the degree to
which Stalinist policy, in spite of declarations to the
contrary, operated under the assumption of a "capitalist stabilization." At that time, in France and Italy,

[1] O. Kuusinen, *Prepare for Power* (New York, Workers
Library Publishers, 1932) p. 40.
[2] *Capitalist Stabilization Has Ended* p. 16.
[3] *Ibid.* p. 22.
[4] *Ibid.* p. 17.

the popular strength of the Communist parties was greater than ever before, and, for the first time, their armed strength seemed adequate for an attempt at seizing power. However, after a few scattered and uncoordinated local putsches, the Communists pursued a policy of cooperation, surrendered their military units, and adhered to a "minimum program" which, even during the subsequent period of the great political strikes, never aimed at revolution as the immediate objective. This strategy may be explained by the weakness of its "mass basis." The national Communist parties were confronted with a situation which defied the traditional concepts of Marxian revolutionary strategy; it soon became apparent that they fought in an entirely different arena. The Allied armies which, together with the legitimate national contingents, confronted the Communists in France, Italy, and Western Germany, unmistakably symbolized the new situation which continued to prevail even after their withdrawal: the "class enemy" could no longer be defeated "on the barricades" in Paris or Lyon or Toulouse, in Milan or Turin or Bologna. Its central positions now were in Washington and New York, in the Allied headquarters and commissions. The civil war had become a matter of international, intercontinental policy in a far more objective sense than that of a dictatorship of the USSR over foreign Communist parties. And in the international constellation at the end of the war, all the odds were in the hands of the Western Allies, specifically, of the United States. To be sure, after the quick Western demobilization, the Soviet armies could have overrun the Continent. But if Marxism played any role at all in Soviet policy decisions, then it influenced Stalin to the extent that he could not envisage the defeat of the capitalist world through a blitzkrieg in Europe, waged by an exhausted and largely destroyed Russia against the practically unimpaired forces of the economically most powerful nation in the world. And Stalin, whose *theory* still stuck to the traditional notion of the aggravating interimperialist contradictions, may well have been surprised at the rapidity with which the "united capitalist front" against Communism reasserted itself after the war (Churchill's speech at Fulton, Missouri, 1946; The "Truman Doctrine" and the Marshall Plan, 1947; Anglo-American negotiations on the Ruhr, 1947).

The Stalinist answer was the doctrine of the "two camps" and the aggressive strategy of 1947-1948 usually associated with Zhdanov. The doctrine comes closest to the open recognition of international capitalist unification[5] and thus closest to discarding the traditional notion of the inner imperialist contradictions—though it actually does neither. For the "two-camp" doctrine includes the Western proletariat in the "anti-imperialist camp" and reiterates the idea of the inevitability of internal and external wars. At about the same time, Varga's cautious recognition of the stabilizing and "productive" function of the capitalist state at this stage was violently rejected. Stalinist foreign policy followed the notion underlying the "two-camp" doctrine that the contradictions between the imperialist and the Communist camp had, for the time being, superseded those between the imperialist powers: Communist rule was tight-

---

[5] See Zhdanov's report to the Cominform conference, September 1947, in *The Strategy and Tactics of World Communism*, House Document No. 619, Supplement I, p. 216. "A new alignment of political forces has arisen." Zhdanov continued by stating that the Western as well as the Far and Middle Eastern countries in the "imperialist camp" follow the leadership of the United States in all main questions.

ened and expanded; loopholes were being closed
(establishment of Cominform, 1947; coup in Czech-
oslovakia, Soviet walkout from the Allied Control
Council in Germany, Berlin blockade, and break
with Tito, 1948). But as early as 1948-1949, the
intransigent Communist strategy in the West was
petering out (failure and abandonment of the political
strikes in France and Italy) and was being replaced
by a new "united-front" policy, which has been retained and stepped up ever since. In the East, the
course was different: the Indian party adhered to an
extreme left strategy until 1950; military operations
in Indo-China were increased; and the war in Korea
began at a time when the Western parties were on
the defensive. During the entire Stalinist period,
Western and Eastern policy were never effectively
correlated; from the time of the dismal consequences
of Stalinist "guidance" in the first phases of the
Chinese revolution, Stalinism seemed to follow rather
than direct the momentum of the "colonial revolutions." There, the new historical agent of the revolution seemed to ripen "naturally," and the peasant
masses, which Lenin had incorporated into revolutionary strategy, seemed to fulfill their function. The
West, the capitalist world, remained the determining
problem for Soviet Marxism.

The Soviet Marxist interpretation of capitalism
centers on the notion of the "general crisis" of the
capitalist system. The crisis itself is seen as expressive of the monopolistic stage of capitalist development—a stage at which the fundamental conflict
between the social character of the productive forces
and their private capitalist utilization has reached
its peak, the last stage before the turning point to
socialism. The foreign policy of the Western nations

and the internal economic and political changes within these nations are explained in terms of this conflict.[6]

The "general crisis," which comprises a whole historical period, is subdivided into two main phases.[7] The second phase, which began with the Second World War, is the sharpening of the crisis. The crisis itself was unleashed by the emergence of the Soviet state and was intensified by its subsequent growth. The specific features of the crisis are the tremendous shrinking of the capitalist world market and the establishment of two parallel but opposed world markets: the capitalist and the "socialist." While the former decreases, the latter increases without depression and dislocation—steadily. Much of the colonial and semicolonial and almost the whole Eastern European market has "broken away" from the capitalist orbit. Moreover, capitalism has not only been cut off from a large part of its former sales market but also from access to many of its former resources of raw materials and cheap labor. The consequence: capitalist production proceeds on an ever-narrowing basis; the difficulties in the extraction and realization of surplus value and, therefore, of profit (already greatly intensified by the "higher organic composi-

[6] For what follows see: M. Rubinshtein, "Osnovnoi ekonomicheskii zakon sovremennogo kapitalizma" (The Basic Economic Law of Contemporary Capitalism), *Voprosy Ekonomiki* (Problems of Economics), 1952, No. 10, pp. 38-55; I. Lemin, "Obostrenie protivorechii i neizbezhnost' voin mezhdu kapitalisticheskimi stranami" (The Sharpening of Contradictions and the Unavoidability of Wars Between Capitalist Countries), *Voprosy Ekonomiki* (Problems of Economics), 1952, No. 12, pp. 34-53; and I. Trakhtenberg, "Osobennosti vosproizvodstva i krizisov v sovremennom kapitalizme" (Characteristics of Production and Crises in Contemporary Capitalism), *Voprosy Ekonomiki* (Problems of Economics), 1952, No. 10, pp. 69-85.

[7] For example, G. V. Kozlov, "Obshchii krizis kapitalisma i ego obostrenie na sovremennom etape" (The General Crisis of Capitalism and Its Sharpening at the Present Stage), *Voprosy Ekonomiki* (Problems of Economics), 1952, No. 4, pp. 68 ff.

tion" of capital, that is—in terms of total capital—
the growing proportion of constant capital and th
decreasing proportion of wages) increase, and forc
the most powerful capitalist groups into a bruta
struggle for their share in the greatly reduced marke
This in turn aggravates the competitive conflict
among the capitalist powers. The struggle for market
assumes, at the late imperialistic stage, the form o
the subjugation of the weaker by the stronger capital
ist powers, culminating in the supremacy of America
imperialism. According to Soviet Marxism, the tren
indicated by Lenin in 1915 has reached its apex. Th
militarization of the economy, the "classical" featur
of imperialism, becomes the "normal" state of affairs
The war economy, while yielding monopolistic sur
plus profits to the top capitalists, depresses the leve
of consumption even in the richest capitalist countries
channels the bulk of capitalist investments into direc
and indirect war industries, and thus increases th
disproportionality between the two main division
of capitalist production. The crisis affects the ver
reproduction of the system.

According to this interpretation, the rise of th
Soviet state has set in motion a chain reaction which
by intensifying the inherent capitalist contradictions
has aggravated the conflicts between the capitalis
powers.[8] This was the theoretical conclusion at th
time of the Sixteenth Party Congress (1930) an

[8] I. Lemin, "Obostrenie protivorechii i neizbezhnost' voi
mezhdu kapitalisticheskimi stranami" (The Sharpening of Con
tradictions and the Unavoidability of Wars between Capitalis
Countries), *Voprosy Ekonomiki* (Problems of Economics)
1952, No. 12, p. 44. This gives the reasons for the violen
reaction against Varga's book, *Izmeneniia v ekonomike kapi
talizma v itoge vtoroi mirovoi voiny* (Changes in the Econom
of Capitalism Resulting from the Second World War) (Mos
cow, Gospolitizdat, 1946). See p. 50 below.

again at the time of the Twentieth Congress (1956). The contradictions which, in the Marxian conception, are inherent in the structure of capitalist production, reassert themselves as the determining ones—contrary to all appearances. Soviet Marxism consistently denies that the international integration of capitalism into one camp against the common enemy can "neutralize" these contradictions. The doctrines of "ultra-imperialism" and "organized capitalism" are again emphatically rejected [9]—as they were forty years ago. The efforts of the American monopolists to establish an American "world trust" have failed. The competitive conflicts within the capitalist orbit sharpen in spite of all integration; the "subjugated" nations balk and strive for reconquering their former position in the world market; Western Germany and Japan reemerge as the most dangerous competitors.[1] The operation of the fundamental economic laws which in Marxian theory determine the course of events thus leads to the growth and explosion of the imperialist contradictions, to military conflicts within the imperialist camp, to the "further deepening of the general crisis of the capitalist system and the approach of its final breakdown." [2]

There are the customary warnings against interpreting the situation in terms of an impending collapse of the capitalist system. Thus, Trakhtenberg states that the increasing difficulty in finding a "way out" of the economic crisis does not mean the "absolute impossibility" of a way out, nor of a prolongation of

[9] I. Lemin, "Obostrenie protivorechii i neizbezhnost' voin mezhdu kapitalisticheskimi stranami" (The Sharpening of Contradictions and the Unavoidability of Wars between Capitalist Countries), *Voprosy Ekonomiki* (Problems of Economics), 1952, No. 12, p. 45.

[1] *Ibid.*, p. 40.

[2] *Ibid.*, p. 53.

the crisis. He points to the inflationary boom of the armament economy prevailing in the capitalist orbit at present, but concludes by reiterating that under the surface of a capitalist "revival" the disintegrating forces of the economic crisis continue to grow.[3]

It is hard to see how the thesis on the sharpening capitalist crisis can provide the pivotal orientation for Soviet Marxism. Repeated for over thirty years in apparent contradiction to the facts, it seems so paradoxical that it is easily dismissed as propaganda. In reality, however, it is a policy-making concept.

In Marxist terminology, the "general crisis" of capitalism (as distinguished from cyclical "depressions") is characterized by the fact that capitalism is no longer capable of functioning in its "classical," "normal" way. The reproduction of capitalist society can no longer be left to (relatively) free enterprise and (relatively) free competition, with the economic laws asserting themselves freely, i.e., in a blind and anarchic manner. The advent of "imperialism" terminates the "classical" period of capitalism and initiates its general crisis; the system can continue to function only through expanding state controls with monopolistic regimentation and domination, wars or preparation for wars, and "intensified exploitation." The "general crisis" does not mean impending collapse and a revolutionary situation, but rather a whole stage of historical development. Thus it means at the same time the continued existence of the capitalist system, and far from excluding "stabilizations," it implies them as its very essence. To Soviet Marxism, the determining factor in the world situation is that the development

[3] I. Trakhtenberg, "Osobennosti vosproizvodstva i krizisov v sovremennom kapitalizme" (Characteristics of Reproduction and Crises in Contemporary Capitalism), *Voprosy Ekonomiki* (Problems of Economics), 1952, No. 10, p. 85.

of socialism *coexists* with and parallels the general crisis of capitalism (instead of *following* it, as envisaged by Marxian theory).

The theses on the tasks of the Comintern and the Communist Party of the Soviet Union (CPSU) in 1925, as adopted by the Fourteenth Conference of the CPSU, speak of "two stabilizations": "Side by side with the partial stabilization of capitalism in bourgeois Europe occurs the indubitable growth of state industry and the strengthening of the socialist elements of the national economy in the USSR." [4] The "partial stabilization of capitalism" to which these theses referred has, according to Soviet theory, since been surpassed by other (and even more lasting) forms of partial stabilization (permanent war economy and the formation of one "imperialist camp"), but the parallelism has remained, and with it the "anomaly" of the development toward socialism. As long as it prevails, it is likely to be the basic factor in the orientation of Soviet policy. In this respect, too, "coexistence" is not merely a statement of fact but also a statement of theory. As such it appeared in Lenin's last political guidance, in the Resolutions of the Fourteenth Party Congress,[5] and it has not been discarded since. Even at the time of the foundation of the Cominform and the corresponding intransigent and "hard" foreign policy, Zhdanov declared that "Soviet foreign policy proceeds from the fact of the coexistence for a long period of the two systems—capitalism and socialism. From this it follows that cooperation between the USSR and

[4] *Vsesoiuznaia Kommunisticheskaia Partiia (B) v rezoliutsiiakh i resheniiakh s"ezdov konferentsii, i plenumov TsK* (The All-Union Communist Party [Bolsheviks] in the Resolutions and Decisions of Congresses, Conferences, and Plenums of the Central Committee) (2 vols.; Moscow, Gospolitizdat, 1936), II, 27.

[5] *Ibid.,* II, 48.

countries with other systems is possible, provided
that the principle of reciprocity is observed and that
obligations once assumed are honoured." [6] Coexistence
makes the avoidance of a military conflict with the
major "imperialist" powers (in Soviet language, a
"policy of peace") the objective that must stand in
the center of the entire foreign policy of the government and must "determine all its basic steps" [7]—not
because of any innate peacefulness of the Soviet
leaders, but because such a conflict would "suspend"
the capitalist contradictions and break the "respite"
which Lenin declared the prerequisite for the survival
of the Soviet state. Just as the "general crisis" of
capitalism marks a whole period of historical development, so does the "respite": it comprises nothing less
than the time required for bringing the civilization
of the backward East up to the level of the advanced
industrial countries. If and when this objective has
been attained, another turning point in the development of Soviet society *and* capitalist society will have
been reached: the commencing of the "second phase"
of socialism would also initiate the reactivation of the
revolutionary potential in the Western world.

Within the framework of this analysis (extremely
crude and superficial if compared with the theoretical
work of Hilferding, Rosa Luxemburg, Lenin, and
Bucharin), modifications and corrections have been
introduced since the time of the Nineteenth Congress
of the CPSU. They appear first as mere changes in
emphasis, trifling enough and not altering the under-

[6] Report at the Cominform conference, September, 1947, in
The Strategy and Tactics of World Communism, House Document No. 619, Supplement I, p. 219.
[7] *Vsesoiuznaia Kommunisticheskaia Partiia (B)* (The All-
Union Communist Party [Bolsheviks]), II, 48.

ying conception. However, they assume greater significance in the context of Soviet developments during the last period of Stalin's life and after his death, as anticipating the possibility of a long term shift in Soviet policy. In this function, they will be discussed in the chapter on "The Transition from Socialism to Communism"; here only a preliminary statement will be given.

The first of these modifications concerns the interimperialist contradictions and those between the Western world and the Soviet camp. Stalinist policy was in its general tendency oriented toward the actual predominance of the East-West conflict over the interimperialist contradictions. Then, at the time of the Nineteenth Congress, a shift became noticeable. It was first announced by Stalin's dictum on a theoretical controversy: he enjoined the party and its spokesmen that the interimperialist contradictions must be considered as the determining ones.[8] "Theoretically," the conflict between the capitalist and socialist camp is greater than the interimperialist conflicts—"in actuality," however, the latter supersede the former. The derogatory contrast between theory and actuality here served as a warning to bring both into line. And indeed, Stalin's statement was followed by a reexamination of the international situation and by a change in domestic and foreign policy which has become ever more conspicuous since his death. The statement suggested the increasing reliance on the "normal" workings of the international political economy, on the inherent difficulties

[8] "Economic Problems of Socialism in the USSR," in *Current Soviet Policies*, ed. by Leo Gruliow (New York, F. A. Praeger, 1953), pp. 7 ff.

of the capitalist system rather than on an assault o
its positions from without.[9]

The second modification pertains to the evaluatio
of contemporary monopoly capitalism, more specif
cally, to that of the growing economic and politic
function of the state in the present era. The questio
whether or not Soviet Marxism could admit th
emergence of "state capitalism" had played a con
siderable role in the postwar discussion. Varga's boo
published in 1946, had been rejected because of it
emphasis on state capitalism, particularly as man
fested in the United States. His notion of the integrat
ing and organizing role of the capitalist state seeme
to vitiate the Marxian thesis of the class characte
of the state and of the impossibility of coping wit
the "anarchic" character of capitalism through central
ized planning. For Soviet Marxism this was not onl
an ideological offense; it threatened to undermin
the theoretical ground of a revolutionary strateg
which denied the long range effectiveness of capitalis
stabilization. In defense of his thesis on the strength
ening of the capitalist state and its changing role i
the capitalist "war economy," Varga had cited Lenin'
proposition on the "transformation of monopoly cap
talism into state-monopoly capitalism" [1] as suggestin
the advent of a new stage of imperialist developmen
which can no longer be interpreted in the sacrosanc
terms of the previous stage. But, in spite of the fac
that in the subsequent discussion of Varga's boo
such transformation was recognized,[2] his positio
was rejected. Only "state-capitalist *tendencies*" wer

[9] For the modification of the thesis on the "inevitability o
war" see pp. 146 f. below.
[1] In the Preface to the first edition of *State and Revolutio*
(New York, International Publishers, 1932), p. 5.
[2] English translation of this discussion in *Soviet Views o
the Post-War World Economy* (Washington, D.C., Publi
Affairs Press, 1948); see especially p. 9.

acknowledged, but no new stage characterized by "state capitalism."[3] Recent articles,[4] however, speak without reservation of "state-monopolistic capitalism" and lay great stress on the positive economic function of the capitalist state—much in the sense used in Varga's previously condemned book. Again, the change in emphasis seems quite insignificant, especially since the same articles stress, in traditional Soviet Marxist terms, the progressing "decay" of monopoly capitalism and the aggravated tensions in its economy, internal as well as international. The possibility of any "ultraimperialist" integration of the capitalist world is just as strongly ridiculed as it was before, and capitalist unity is pictured as permeated with intense competitive conflicts on a reduced world market. However, these well-known clichés of Stalinist doctrine now appear within a programmatic reevaluation of capitalism. The flat rejection of one of the most intensively publicized theses in Stalin's last article (namely, the shrinking of production in the United States, Britain, and France),[5] the warning against

[3] E. Varga, "The Decline of British Imperialism," in *Current Digest of the Soviet Press*, II, No. 32 (September 23, 1950), pp. 3 ff. (condensed from *Voprosy Ekonomiki* [Problems of Economics], 1950, No. 4, pp. 48-71).

[4] V. Cheprakov, "Burshuaznye ekonomisty i gosudarstvenno-monopoliticheskii kapitalizm" (Bourgeois Economists and State-Monopoly Capitalism), *Voprosy Ekonomiki* (Problems of Economics), 1955, No. 9, pp. 134-47; and V. Cheprakov, "Leninkaia teoriia neravnomernosti razvitiia kapitalizma i obostrenie mezhimperialisticheskikh protivorechii v poslevoennyi period" (The Leninist Theory of the Unequal Development of Capitalism and the Sharpening of the Imperialistic Contradictions in the Post-War Period), *Voprosy Ekonomiki* (Problems of Economics), 1956, No. 4, pp. 30-47.

[5] Mikoyan, at the Twentieth Party Congress, in *XX S"ezd Kommunisticheskoi Partii Sovetskogo Soiuza* (The Twentieth Congress of the Communist Party of the Soviet Union), I, 323. Although Stalin's name was mentioned specifically in the broadcast of Mikoyan's address, it was omitted in the official report of the Congress.

taking a "simplified view of Lenin's theses on th
decay of imperialism,"[6] the admission that sinc
"the time of Lenin the world situation has fundamen
tally changed"[7]—all these in the context of th
discussion of the international situation—point to
reformulation of some of the sacrosanct tenets of th
Stalinist era. The former refusal to recognize a "nev
stage" of capitalist development is at least implicitl
invalidated when it is acknowledged that the improv
ing conditions of the workers and the "growth o
production in capitalist countries" (though they di
not take place "on a sound economic foundation"
are due to "basic factors." They are said to be chiefl
the following:[8] (1) the "militarization of the economy
with its influence on the general level of output; (2
the expansion of the capitalist market, which wa
rendered possible by the defeat of Germany an
Japan and by the introduction of the Marshall Plan
(3) the long overdue renewal of fixed capital an
modernization of equipment; (4) intensified "exploita
tion of the working class," mainly through rationali
zation and the ensuing higher productivity of labor
These factors are, of course, operating predominantl
in the United States, and the fact that they are nov
so heavily emphasized in the most authoritativ
Soviet Marxist statements is tantamount to a revalua
tion of the strength of American capitalism. The draf
resolution of the American Communist Party add
another decisive factor of strength: "The ruling clas
was not so hard pressed as to be unable to continu

[6] Khrushchev, in *ibid.*, I, 15.
[7] Mikoyan, in *ibid.*, I, 323.
[8] Khrushchev, in *ibid.*, I, 15-16, and Khrushchev's speech o
November 6, 1957 (as broadcast by Moscow Home Service, p
A-47).

ts established method of governmental rule." [9] In Marxian theory, these economic and political factors are indeed "basic" enough to render the "repeated estimates of impending economic crisis" "harmful" and "unrealistic." [1]

However, it is important to note again the "positive" aspects of this revaluation for the Soviet state. Quite apart from the "unsound foundation" of the stabilized capitalist system, the latter would live up to Engels's[2] and Lenin's[3] notion of the "last stage" of capitalism. Fully developed "state-monopolistic capitalism" [4] would better than mere state-capitalist "tendencies" qualify for the historical level at which capitalism reaches its unsurpassable "limits."

The "General Crisis" and the Western Proletariat

The extent to which the Soviet Marxist argument applies the traditional Marxian categories to the analysis of Western society becomes especially clear in the evaluation of the Western proletariat. During the Stalinist period, Soviet Marxism denied the existence of an economic basis for any long-range stabilization of capitalism; the post-Stalinist modifications come close to recognizing such a basis (although

[9] *New York Times*, September 23, 1956.
[1] *Ibid.*
[2] "Anti-Dühring," in *A Handbook of Marxism*, ed. by E. Burns (New York, International Publishers, 1935), pp. 292 ff.
[3] *Imperialism: The Highest Stage of Capitalism* (New York, International Publishers, 1933), pp. 7, 14, 15.
[4] Its main features are summarized in Cheprakov, "Leninskaia teoriia neravnomernosti razvitiia kapitalizma i obostrenie mezhimperialisticheskikh protivorechii v poslevoennyi period" (The Leninist Theory of the Unequal Development of Capitalism and the Sharpening of the Imperialistic Contradictions in the Post-War Period), *Voprosy Ekonomiki* (Problems of Economics), 1956, No. 4, pp. 30-47.

they regard it as "unsound"). In both cases, however
Soviet *theory* denies any fundamental change in the
class situation. The Western proletariat continues to
be considered as the revolutionary class (though not
in a "revolutionary situation"), and, by the same token
as the final disruptive force in the general crisis. The
very same Resolution of the Fourteenth Party Con
gress which proclaimed a policy of "peaceful coexist
ence" as the center of Soviet foreign policy demanded
a strengthening by all means of the "union between
the proletariat of the USSR, as basis for the world
revolution, and the Western European proletariat and
the subjugated peoples." [5] In his concluding remark
to the Nineteenth Congress, Stalin harked back to
this union by recalling the role of the Soviet pro
letariat as the "shock brigade" of the "world revolu
tionary and workers' movement." [6] The Twentieth
Congress reiterated the thesis that the laboring masses
in the capitalist countries were the strongest force in
the struggle against imperialist aggression. The recon
ciliation of large sections of labor with the capitalis
system and the increase in their standard of living
are explained in terms of "relative impoverishment."
Lenin's notion of the "corruption" of the "labor aris
tocracy" is retained with slight modifications: the
challenge of Soviet socialism, the growth of world
communism, and the power of organized labor in the
capitalist countries compel the monopoly capitalist
to "make a series of social concessions, whose exten
and duration depend on the level of the struggle of
the working class in the capitalist countries." [7]

[5] *Vsesoiuznaia Kommunisticheskaia Partiia (B)* (All-Union
Communist Party [Bolsheviks]), II, 48.
[6] *Current Soviet Policies*, p. 235.
[7] V. Cheprakov, "Nekotorye voprosy sovremennogo kapita
lizma" (Some Questions on Contemporary Capitalism), *Kom*

But while Soviet theory continues to be concerned with the sharpening class struggle in the capitalist countries, Soviet policy has adjusted itself to the factual situation and has put the Western proletariat "on ice" until the turning point is reached at which it will be reactivated as a revolutionary force. The lumping together of the proletariat with other "peace-loving" social groups indicates recognition of the underlying historical tendency. The "revolutionary class" assumes the features of democratic reformism. Soviet Marxism makes use of a well-known theoretical concept in order to explain and justify this tendency.

According to Soviet Marxism, the failure of the Central European revolutions and the subjugation of formerly independent capitalist countries under American hegemony threw the revolutionary development in Western Europe back to a stage prior to the "bourgeois-democratic revolution." Monopoly-capitalist domination undermines national sovereignties, democratic rights, and liberal ideologies; the great progressive achievements of the ascending bourgeoisie have been betrayed by the monopolistic bourgeoisie. Under these circumstances, it becomes the task of the proletariat and the Communist parties in the subjugated countries to lift and carry the "banner of bourgeois democratic freedoms," of "national independence and national sovereignty" [8]—in other words, to take over, or rather to resume, at a higher stage, the historical role of the progressive against the reactionary bourgeoisie. The "minimum program" of the Western Communist parties thus conforms to the Soviet evaluation of the international constellation and

munist (Communist), 1956, No. 1 (January). See also Khrushchev's speech of November 6, 1957 (as broadcast by Moscow Home Service, p. A-47).

[8] Stalin, in *Current Soviet Policies*, p. 236.

must be considered a long-range feature rather than
a brief expediency. As such the "minimum program"
is incorporated into the ritual formulas of Soviet
Marxism: "Defense of national sovereignty and the
struggle against the threat of foreign enslavement
have become vitally important for the working class
and the working people of all countries in the present
epoch." [9] Not "proletarian solidarity" but the sponsor-
ship of the "bourgeois-democratic" program provides
the tenuous link between the Soviet state and the
masses that follow the national Communist parties (a
good index for the change in the historical "subject")
and this program is used as a lever for activating the
interimperialist contradictions.

The "united-front" policy[1] belongs to the same conception. It is dictated by the objective conditions of
"organized capitalism" which has made large sections
of the laboring classes into beneficiaries of the new
prosperity and thereby has seemed to provide a late
justification for reformist and antirevolutionary attitudes. If, as Marxism has never ceased to claim, the
effectiveness of the revolution depends on winning
over the majority, not only of the proletariat but of
the people, then Communist strategy has to be adjusted to the conditions under which the majority is
not revolutionary. And in so far as the nonrevolutionary conditions pertain to a whole stage of the capitalist
development, the united-front policy is a fundamental
stratagem which cannot be discarded at the discretion
of the leadership. Indeed, the united front has been

[9] P. Fedoseev, "Socialism and Patriotism," in *Current Digest
of the Soviet Press*, V, No. 28 (August 22, 1953), 4 (condensed from *Kommunist* [Communist], No. 9 [June, 1953]
pp. 12-28).
[1] The "united front" is discussed here only in its function in
the West, not in the Communist orbit, where it has a very
different significance.

an objective of Soviet policy at least ever since 1934, although the emphasis and scope of the effort have changed several times. What is decisive for the evaluation is not whether the united front aims at the rank and file, or also at the leadership of the socialist parties and trade unions, not whether it aims beyond these groups at some or all of the "bourgeois parties," but whether the policy is likely to alter the very character of the Communist parties. Even the problem of the success of the policy is of minor importance. Since the response of the would-be noncommunist allies is determined by the degree of the functioning of Western society, the united front is bound to remain abortive and "localized" as long as this society remains a going concern. If this should no longer be the case, the united-front policy would be all but superfluous. However, the mere sustained *effort* to achieve a united front may make the Communist parties in important aspects the political heirs of the Social Democratic parties.[2] As the latter tend to lose the working-class character and approach that of the middle-class parties, a vacuum may arise in which the Communists may appear as the sole representatives of working-class interests—interests which in turn would call for nonrevolutionary representation. A tendency in this direction is noticeable in France and in Italy, and the declarations, at the Twentieth Congress of the CPSU, on the possibility of a parliamentary way to socialism[3] recall substantially Engels's preface to Marx's *Class Struggles in France*, which was for a long time taken

[2] See p. 225 below. See also the Joint Communiqué of Communist and Workers' Parties, New York *Times*, November 22, 1957.

[3] Khrushchev, at the Twentieth Party Congress, in *XX S"ezd Kommunisticheskoi Partii Sovetskogo Soiuza* (The Twentieth Congress of the Communist Party of the Soviet Union, I, 38 ff.; Mikoyan, in *ibid.*, pp. 312 ff.

as guidance for Social Democratic strategy. We may
venture the suggestion that this tendency would be
much stronger were it not for the identification of the
interests of the national Communist parties with that
of the USSR and for the political countermeasures
against the Communist parties.

In view of the constancy of the main elements of
Soviet Marxism, the question must be asked whether
there is a "break" between Leninism and Stalinism.
The differences between the first years of the Bolshevik Revolution and the fully developed Stalinist
state are obvious; they readily appear as the steady
growth of totalitarianism and authoritarian centralization, as the growth of the dictatorship not of but over
the proletariat and the peasantry. But if the dialectical
law of the turn from quantity into quality was ever
applicable, it was in the transition from Leninism
(after the October Revolution) to Stalinism. The "re-
tardation" of the revolution in the West and the
stabilization of capitalism made for qualitative changes
in the structure of Soviet society. Lenin tried to counter the isolation of the revolution in a backward
country by establishing the priority of industrialization
over socialist liberation (it is epitomized in his definition of socialism as electrification plus Soviet power)
—the priority of the Soviet state over Soviet workers.[4]
Lenin died before the ascent of fascism in Germany;
from then on, the "respite" for which he had striven
seemed to be of an ever shorter duration. Thus, Stalin
accelerated the program of "civilization" which Lenin
had made the prerequisite for the preservation of the
Soviet system. The height of the Stalinist terror coin-

---

[4] For the most striking examples of this attitude (then fully
endorsed by Trotsky), see Carr, *The Bolshevik Revolution*, II,
passim, especially pp. 93 f., 188 f., 213-16.

cided with the consolidation of the Hitler regime. At the outbreak of the Second World War, Soviet civilization had progressed far enough to withstand the most powerful war machine of an advanced industrial country. Postwar reconstruction was amazingly fast in view of the unprecedented destruction—but so was the reconstruction in the other camp. Soviet policy at the end of the war, with its series of occupations and "revolutions from above," regardless of the constellation of the indigenous social forces in the respective countries, indicates that Stalin did not believe that a revolutionary system was maturing in Europe, or that the Soviet state could depend for its long-range preservation on the colonial revolutions. Lenin's prescription was still valid, and set the overriding objective of the Soviet state during the "first phase" of socialism. It has been ritualized in the formula, *"to outstrip the economic level of the chief capitalist countries."* [5] Soviet society continued to grow; the development of socialist production continued to increase the material and technical potential while repressing the human potential.

But the very success of Stalinist civilization leads to an impasse, which is clearly defined in the Marxist-Leninist theory of imperialism. According to this theory, the war economy provides an outlet for the aggravating inherent contradictions of capitalism, although the capitalist consolidation thus created is

[5] Stalin at the Eighteenth Party Congress in 1939, in *Leninism* (New York, International Publishers, 1942), p. 448; and again after the war in his speech of February 9, 1946, in *Pravda*, February 10, 1946. The formula also concludes N. Voznesenskii's *Voennaia Ekonomika SSSR v Period Otechestvennoi Voiny* (The Military Economy of the USSR in the Period of the Fatherland War) (Moscow, Gospolitizdat, 1947); it was not because of this conclusion that the book was repudiated.

precarious and short-lived and bound to explode in
wars between the competing imperialist countries.
However, if and when there is a "common enemy"
outside the capitalist world, whose growing power and
expansion requires the maintenance of a "permanent"
war or preparedness economy in which the imperialist
powers unite, while at the same time technological
progress enables capitalism to maintain this economy
without noticeably reducing the standard of living
(perhaps even increasing it!), then a situation prevails
where the very growth of the Soviet orbit seems to
sustain the unity and stability of the "imperialist"
orbit. The former cannot break this impasse without
fundamentally altering its policy—and this in turn is
conditional upon a corresponding advance of Soviet
society. Such a change in policy—aiming at the dissolution of the "war economy" on which the capitalist
stabilization is held to rest—presupposes that the
Soviet state has attained a level of competitive strength
which enables it to "relax" its intransigent and aggressive strategy. Only such a relaxation, sustained
systematically and for a long time, could possibly
shatter the international capitalist stabilization and
revert the capitalist system to that "normality" in which
the internal contradictions are supposed to ripen and
ultimately to explode. The ideological and political
changes, which began at the time of the Nineteenth
Congress and gained momentum during 1955-1956
indicated an impending shift in policy. Its timing was
not a matter of discretion by the Soviet leadership,
nor was Stalin's death the decisive factor. The latter
must rather be seen in the fulfillment of the fundamental prerequisite for restoring the "normal" capi-
talist-socialist dynamic, namely, the attainment of the
level of advanced industrial civilization for Soviet

society. If, as we propose, the recent policy changes suggest that, in the Soviet Marxist evaluation, this prerequisite has now been established, then these changes would usher in an essentially new stage in international Communist developments.

The following chapters will survey the main features of Soviet Marxism during the Stalinist period and try to connect them with the underlying trend in the construction of Soviet society.

3

THE NEW RATIONALITY

We shall begin with the attempt to define, in a preliminary way, the rationale of the civilization of "socialism in one country," that is to say, the principles which govern its construction and its inner dynamic. In doing so, we accept as guidance neither the term "socialism," nor its simple negation, nor "totalitarianism" and its synonyms—not socialism because the validation of the concept depends on agreement on definition and can even then only be the result of the examination; not totalitarianism because the notion is applicable to a wide variety of social systems with different and antagonistic structures. We shall rather try to arrive at the identification of these principles by assembling those features of the construction of Soviet society which have remained generally constant throughout all stages, regressions, and modifications. They may be restated, in summary form, as follows:

1. Total industrialization, on the basis of nationalized production, with priority of "main division I" (production of the means of production)

2. Progressive collectivization of agriculture aiming at the ultimate transformation of collective into state property

3. General mechanization of labor, extension of

"polytechnic" training, leading to "equalization" between urban and rural occupations

4. Gradual rise in the general standard of living
conditional on the maintenance of the goals set in
Points 1-3

5. Building up of a universal work morale, competitive efficiency, elimination of all transcendent psychological and ideological elements ("Soviet realism")

6. Preservation and strengthening of the state, military, managerial, and party machinery as the vehicle
for these processes (1-5)

7. Transition to the distribution of the social product
according to individual needs after attainment of the
goals set in Points 1-5

The goals are conditional upon the attainment of
the productivity level of the advanced industrial countries; this is the termination point for the presently
prevailing trends. Beyond this point, new and qualitatively different trends are stipulated; they will be
indicated in Chapter 8, in an attempt to evaluate the
prospects of the "transition to communism."

The following principles refer to the Soviet Marxist
interpretation of this transition:

1. The development of Soviet society from socialism
to communism takes place as the dialectical process
of unfolding internal and external contradictions.

2. The internal contradictions can be solved rationally, without "explosion," on the basis of the
socialist economy under the control and direction of
the Soviet state.

3. The fundamental internal contradiction, which
provides the motor power for the transition to communism, is that between the constantly growing
productive forces and the lagging relations of production. Its rational and controlled development makes

for a gradual and administrative transition to communism.

4. The gradual transition to communism occurs under conditions of capitalist encirclement (environment). The external contradictions involved in this situation can be finally solved only at the international level—through a socialist revolution in some of the advanced capitalist countries.

5. This solution is itself a long-range process, covering a whole period of capitalist and socialist development. The weakness of the revolutionary potential in the capitalist world and the still prevailing backwardness of the Soviet orbit necessitate a new extended "respite" and "coexistence" of the two systems.

6. The Soviet Union must preserve this respite by utilizing conflicts among the imperialist powers,[1] avoiding a war with them, and discouraging revolutionary experiments ("seizure of power") in the advanced capitalist countries.

7. The solution of the external contradictions will ripen through (*a*) the inherent capitalist and intercapitalist contradictions, which will make the proletariat again the historical agent of the revolution; (*b*) the growing economic, political, and strategic power of the USSR.

8. The "main reserves" supporting these basic revolutionary forces are the semiproletarian and petty peasant masses in the developed countries, and the

---

[1] The last two points summarize Lenin's conception for the "third historic phase of the Russian Revolution" (beginning with the victory of the October Revolution and lasting into the present), as paraphrased by Stalin. See Stalin, *Sochineniia* (Works), (13 vols.; Moscow, Gospolitizdat, 1946-51), VI, 153; also L. F. Shorichev, *Voprosy strategii i taktiki v trudakh I. V. Stalina perioda 1921-1925 godov* (Problems of Strategy and Tactics in the Writings of J. V. Stalin, 1921-1925) (Moscow, *Pravda*, 1950).

liberation movements in the colonies and dependent countries.

The social process guided by these principles is more than the industrialization of the backward areas of the East on the basis of nationalization under totalitarian administration. What is happening here extends beyond the borders of the Communist orbit. Communist industrialization proceeds through "skipping" and telescoping whole historical periods. The fundamental difference between Western and Soviet society is paralleled by a strong trend toward assimilation. Both systems show the common features of late industrial civilization—centralization and regimentation supersede individual enterprise and autonomy; competition is organized and "rationalized"; there is joint rule of economic and political bureaucracies; the people are coordinated through the "mass media" of communication, entertainment industry, education. If these devices prove to be effective, democratic rights and institutions might be granted by the constitution and maintained without the danger of their abuse in opposition to the system. Nationalization, the abolition of private property in the means of production, does not, by itself, constitute an essential distinction as long as production is centralized and controlled over and above the population. Without initiative and control "from below" by the "immediate producers," nationalization is but a technological-political device for increasing the productivity of labor, for accelerating the development of the productive forces and for their control from above (central planning)—a change in the mode of domination, streamlining of domination, rather than prerequisite for its abolition. By abrogating the individual as the autonomous economic and political subject, certain "obsolete" brakes on the development of the productive forces are eliminated. Individual units of production (material and intellectual) are no longer adequate instrumentalities for integrating society; technological progress and mass production shatter the individualistic forms in which progress operated during the liberalist era.

But, at the same time, technical progress and growing productivity threaten to counteract this trend. Increasing social capacity and wealth militate against the repressive organization and division of labor. Awareness of these countertrends manifests itself in the recent policy changes and in the increased Soviet Marxist emphasis on the necessary transition to the "second phase of socialism," which will be discussed below.[2]

The Soviet system seems to be another example of a late-comer "skipping" several developmental stages after a long period of protracted backwardness, joining and running ruthlessly ahead of a general trend in late industrial society. The skipped stages are those of enlightened absolutism and liberalism, of free competitive enterprise, of matured middle-class culture with its individualistic and humanitarian ideologies. The effort to catch up, in record time and from a state of backwardness, with the level of the advanced industrial countries led to the construction and utilization of a huge productive apparatus within a system of domination and regimentation incompatible with individualistic rationality and liberalism. Here lie the roots of the relentless struggle of Soviet Marxism against the liberal and idealist elements of "bourgeois ideologies"; the struggle reflects the societal organization of the productive forces as instruments of control rather than liberation.

[2] See Chapter 8.

The idea of Reason which was representative of modern Western civilization centered on the autonomy of the *Ego Cogitans*, whose independent thinking discovered and implemented the laws of the rational organization of nature and society. The Ego was itself subject to the objective laws of nature—but subjective and objective Reason were to coincide in a society that had mastered nature and transformed it into a practically inexhaustible material for the development of human needs and faculties. Attainment of this goal called for the emancipation of the individual as long as the state, the established authorities, were an impediment to technical and economic progress. The latter was expected to result from the reasonably free functioning of a multitude of individual enterprises (economic, political, cultural), and the rationality of the whole was to assert itself through the competitive process of these individual units. This process required a high degree of individual autonomy, foresight, calculability, perspicacity—qualities that had to be acquired not only in the actual business of living but also in the preparation for it: in the family, in school, in the privacy of thinking and feeling. Social progress thus depended to a large extent on the autonomy of the individual, that is, on the distinction and tension between subjective and objective Reason, and on a solution of this tension in such a way that objective Reason (the social need and the social interest) preserved and developed subjective Reason (the individual need and the individual interest).

Technological progress and the development of large industry contained two (antagonistic) tendencies which had a decisive impact on this process: (1) mechanization and rationalization of labor could free an ever greater quantum of individual energy (and time) from the material work process and allow the expenditure of this energy and time for the free play of human faculties beyond the realm of material production; and (2) the same mechanization and rationalization generated attitudes of standardized conformity and precise submission to the machine which required adjustment and reaction rather than autonomy and spontaneity.[3] If nationalization and centralization of the industrial apparatus goes hand in hand with counteracting the first of these tendencies, i.e., with the subjugation and enforcement of labor as a full-time occupation, progress in industrialization is tantamount to progress in domination: attendance to the machine, the scientific work process, becomes totalitarian, affecting all spheres of life. The technological perfection of the productive apparatus dominates the rulers and the ruled while sustaining the distinction between them. Autonomy and spontaneity are confined to the level of efficiency and performance within the established pattern. Intellectual effort becomes the business of engineers, specialists, agents. Privacy and leisure are handled as relaxation from and preparation for labor in conformity with the apparatus. Dissent is not only a political crime but also technical stupidity, sabotage, mistreatment of the machine. Reason is nothing but the rationality of the whole: the uninterrupted functioning and growth of the apparatus. The experience of the harmony between the individual and the general interest, between the human and the social need, remains a mere promise.

The Soviet Marxist self-interpretation of this rationality may serve to elucidate its function. According to this interpretation, the October Revolution has

[3] Thorstein Veblen, *The Instinct of Workmanship* (New York, B. W. Huebsch, 1922), pp. 306 ff.

created a "conformity" between production relations
and the "character of the productive forces" which
eliminates the conflict between the individual and
society, between the particular and the common interest. Consequently, Reason ceases to be split into
its subjective and objective manifestations; it is no
longer antagonistic to and beyond reality, a mere
"idea"—but is realized in the society itself. This
society, defined as socialist in terms of Marxian theory,
becomes the sole standard of truth and falsehood;
there can be no transcendence in thought and action,
no individual autonomy because the Nomos of the
whole is the true Nomos. To transcend that which is,
to set subjective reason against state reason, to appeal
to higher norms and values, belongs to the prerogatives
of class society, where the Nomos of society is not the
Nomos of its individuals. In contrast, Soviet society
institutionalizes the real interests of the individuals—
by this token, it contains all standards of true and
false, right and wrong. "Soviet realism" is not a mere
matter of philosophy and aesthetics; it is the general
pattern of intellectual and practical behavior demanded by the structure of Soviet society.

To be sure, outside the validity of Soviet Marxism,
where the equation of the Soviet state with a free and
rational society is not accepted, this notion of the
"realization of Reason" is itself an ideology. Since in
actuality the individual interest is still antagonistic to
the interest of the whole, since nationalization is not
socialization, the rationality of Soviet realism appears
as utterly irrational, as terroristic conformity. However, to stop the evaluation of the new Soviet rationality at this point would be to overlook its decisive
function. For what is irrational if measured from without the system is rational within the system. The key

propositions of Soviet Marxism have the function of announcing and commanding a definite practice, apt to create the facts which the propositions stipulate. They claim no truth-value of their own but proclaim a preestablished truth which is to be realized through a certain attitude and behavior. They are pragmatic directives for action. For example, Soviet Marxism is built around a small number of constantly recurring and rigidly canonized statements to the effect that Soviet society is a socialist society without exploitation, a full democracy in which the constitutional rights of all citizens are guaranteed and enforced; or, on the other side, that present-day capitalism exists in a state of sharpening class struggle, depressed living standards, unemployment, and so forth. Thus formulated and taken by themselves, these statements are obviously false—according to Marxian as well as non-Marxian criteria. But within the context in which they appear, their falsity does not invalidate them, for, to Soviet Marxism, their verification is not in the given facts, but in "tendencies," in a historical process in which the commanded political practice will *bring about* the desired facts.

The value of these statements is pragmatic rather than logical, as is clearly suggested by their syntactical structure. They are unqualified, inflexible formulas calling for an unqualified, inflexible response. In endless repetition, the same noun is always accompanied by the same adjectives and participles; the noun "governs" them immediately and directly so that whenever it occurs they follow "automatically" in their proper place. The same verb always "moves" the proposition in the same direction, and those addressed by the proposition are supposed to move the same way. These statements do not attribute a predicate to a subject (in the sense of formal or of dialectical logic); they do not develop the subject in its specific relations—all these cognitive processes lie outside the propositional context, i.e., in the "classics" of Marxism, and the routine statements only recall what is pre-established. They are to be "spelled," learned mechanically, monotonously, and literally; they are to be performed like a ritual which accompanies the realizing action. They are to recall and sustain the required practice. Taken by themselves they are no more committed to the truth than are orders or advertisements: their "truth" is in their effect. Soviet Marxism here shares in the decline of language and communication in the age of mass societies. It is senseless to treat the propositions of the official ideology at the cognitive level: they are a matter of practical, not of theoretical reason. If propositions lose their cognitive value to their capacity of bringing about a desired effect, that is to say, if they are to be understood as directives for a specific behavior, then *magical* elements gain ascendancy over comprehending thought and action. The difference between illusion and reality becomes just as obliterated as that between truth and falsehood if illusions guide a behavior that shapes and changes reality. With respect to its actual effect on primitive societies, magic has been described as a "body of purely practical acts, performed as means to an end." [4] The description may well be applied to formally theoretical propositions. The official language itself assumes magical character.

However, the contemporary reactivation of magical features in communication is far from primitive. The irrational elements of magic enter into the system of

[4] Bronislaw Malinowski, *Magic, Science and Religion* (Anchor Books; New York, Doubleday, 1954), p. 70.

scientifically planned and practiced administration—
they become part of the scientific management of
society. Moreover, the magical features of Soviet
theory are turned into an instrument for rescuing the
truth. While the ritual formulas, severed from their
original cognitive context, thus serve to provide unquestioned directives for unquestioned mass behavior,
they retain, in a hypostatized form, their historical
substance. The rigidity with which they are celebrated
is to preserve the purity of this substance in the face
of an apparently contradicting reality and to enforce
verification in the face of apparently contradicting
facts which make the preestablished truth into a paradox. It defies reason; it seems absurd. But the absurdity
of Soviet Marxism has an objective ground: it reflects
the absurdity of a historical situation in which the
realization of the Marxian promises appeared—only
to be delayed again—and in which the new productive forces are again used as instruments for productive
repression. The ritualized language preserves the
original content of Marxian theory as a truth that
must be believed and enacted against all evidence
to the contrary: the people must do and feel and think
as if their state were the reality of that reason, freedom, and justice which the ideology proclaims, and
the ritual is to assure such behavior. The practice
guided by it indeed moves large underprivileged
masses on an international scale. In this process, the
original promises of Marxian theory play a decisive
part. The new form of Marxian theory corresponds to
its new historical agent—a backward population which
is to become what it "really" is: a revolutionary force
which changes the world. The ritualization of this
theory has kept it alive against the power of factual
refutation and communicated it, in ideological form,

to a backward and suppressed population which is to
be whipped into political action, contesting and chal-
lenging advanced industrial civilization. In its magical
use, Marxian theory assumes a new rationality.

The paradoxical character of Soviet rationality is
not confined to its own orbit; it also pertains to statements referring to the capitalist orbit. To be sure,
straight falsehood may often be attributed to mere
propaganda requirements. But here too, the recurrent
pattern of falsehood beyond plausibility suggests the
intent of defiance: the concerted struggle with facts
which, measured against the world historical "truth,"
are accidental and to be negated. If, for example,
Pravda's special New York correspondent reports[5] that
in the card catalogue of the New York Public Library
he did not find a single book "about Stalingrad or the
Soviet army in general," the fact that the New York
Public Library's catalogue contains about "two dozen
cards bearing directly on the Battle of Stalingrad" and
"about 500 cards under 'Army, Russia'" is, for the
Soviet reporter, "negated" by the essential context of
systematic American hostility to the Soviet Union. Or,
if William Z. Foster's *History of the Communist Party
of the United States*, published in 1952—at a time
when the party was practically without any popular
support, its leadership in jail, its membership a negligi-
ble quantity—ends with a chapter headed "The Party
of the Working Class and the Nation," and with a
section headed "The Progress of the Communist Party,"
then the shattering unreality of these statements is
itself part of their function: to refuse submission to
the facts, to uphold and accomplish the true nature
of the party as the "Leninist mass party" against its
inadequate factual existence.

[5] New York *Times*, February 2, 1953.

Hypostatized into a ritual pattern, Marxian theory becomes ideology. But its content and function distinguish it from the "classical" forms of ideology: it is not "false consciousness," [6] but rather consciousness of falsehood, a falsehood which is "corrected" in the context of the "higher truth" represented by the objective historical interest. This tends to cancel the ideological freedom of consciousness and to assimilate ideology with the basis as part of consciously directed social action. As the contrast between ideology and reality sharpens with the growing contrast between the productive potential of society and its repressive use, the previously free elements of the ideology are subjected to administrative control and direction. The weakening of the relative independence of ideologies from established social needs, the ossification of their content, is characteristic of the present stage of civilization. In its ossified form, emptied of its meaning which was critical of and antagonistic to the established society, the ideology becomes a tool of domination. If ideas like human liberty and reason or individual autonomy of thought are no longer comprehended in their still unfulfilled claim but are items in the routine equipment of newspapers, statesmen, entertainers, and advertisers who betray them daily in their business of perpetuating the status quo, then the progressive notions of the ideology are deprived of their transcendent function and made into clichés of desired behavior.

The decline of independent thought vastly increases the power of words—their magical power, with whose destruction the process of civilization had once begun.

[6] Engels, Letter to Franz Mehring, July 14, 1893, in Marx and Engels, *Selected Works* (2 vols.; Moscow, Foreign Languages Publishing House, 1949-50), II, 451.

Protected against the intellectual effort which trace
the way back from the words to the ideas they onc
expressed, the words become weapons in the hand c
an administration against which the individual is con
pletely powerless. Through the means of mass con
munication, they transmit the objectives of th
administration, and the underlying population r
sponds with the expected behavior.

The rationality which had accompanied the progres
of Western civilization had developed in the tensio
between thought and its object: truth and falsehoo
were sought in the relation between the comprehenc
ing subject and its world, and logic was the compr
hensible development of this relation, expressed i
propositions. Just as the object of thought was take
as something by and in itself (no matter how insepar;
ble from thought), so the subject was held to b
something "for itself"—free to discover the truth abov
its object—and especially the still hidden truth: i
unrealized potentialities. Cognitive freedom was hel
to be an essential part of practical freedom, of th
ability to act in accordance with the truth, to realiz
the subjective and objective potentialities. Where th
relation between subject and object no longer prevail
traditional logic has lost its ground. Truth and fals
hood then are no longer qualities of cognitive propos
tions but of a preestablished and predefined state c
affairs to which thought and action are to be geare
Logic then is measured by the adequacy of suc
thought and action to attain the predetermined goa

4

SOCIALISM
IN ONE COUNTRY?

The new rationality, which the preceding chapter tried to identify, characterizes the atmosphere in which the construction of Soviet society takes place. More specifically, this rationality pertains to the paradoxical nature of Soviet society, where the most methodical system of domination is to prepare the ground for freedom, where the policy of suppression is justified as the policy of liberation. We did not accept the assumption that Soviet Marxism is simply a super-imposed ideology, serving as a prop for the regime; nor did we accept the opposite assumption that Soviet society is a socialist society in the Marxian sense. Therefore we cannot explain the paradox merely as the plain contrast between ideology and reality. The paradox rather seems to reflect the construction of Soviet society under the "anomalous" conditions of coexistence.

We have stressed that as long as control over the means of production and over the distribution of the product is not vested in the "immediate producers" themselves, that is, as long as there is no control and initiative "from below," nationalization is a mere instrument of more effective domination as well as industrialization, of increasing and manipulating the productivity of labor within the framework of mass societies. In this respect, Soviet society follows the general trend of late industrial civilization. However, the question must be asked whether, in spite of this fact, Soviet nationalization, under the historical condition of its progress, does not possess an inner dynamic which may counteract the repressive tendencies and transform the structure of Soviet society—regardless of the real or alleged policies and objectives of the leadership. Within the scope of this study, the dynamic will be traced only in so far as it is reflected in the development of Soviet Marxism, and the discussion will be confined to some selected conceptions which seem to be particularly illuminating. We shall take the conception of "socialism in one country," the dialectic of the Soviet state governed by this policy conception, certain changes in the ideology, and finally the "transition from socialism to communism," in which this dynamic culminates.

The doctrine of "socialism in one country," which provided the general framework for Soviet Marxism during the Stalinist period,[1] also serves to provide a world-historical justification for the repressive functions of the Soviet state. The doctrine has retained throughout its dependence on the international development: the initial isolation of the Bolshevik Revolution, the confinement of socialism to backward areas, and the reconsolidation of capitalism on an intercontinental scale are held responsible for the internal as well as external contradictions which plague Soviet

[1] M. M. Rozental, *Marksistskii dialekticheskii metod* (Marxist Dialectical Method) (Moscow, Gospolitizdat, 1951), pp. 57, 108, and *passim*.

society. Stalinist doctrine holds that the former can be solved by and within the Soviet Union, through the "directing" role of the state, while the latter can be ultimately removed only through the international process[2]—through revolution within the capitalist world. In reality, however, the external contradictions perpetuate the internal ones and vice versa, so that the distinction loses its finality; by its own development, "socialism in one country" dissolves into a larger conception which reestablishes the essential links between the construction of Soviet society and the capitalist development.

The Soviet Marxist designation of the internal contradictions varies with the various stages of the development. Chiefly they are defined in terms of the contradiction between the proletariat and the peasantry,[3] between the socialist state and "our own bourgeoisie," [4] between kulaks and poor peasants, mental and physical labor, "old consciousness" and socialist mentality.[5] Their basis is identified as the contradiction between the growth of the productive forces and the lagging level of consumption. The external contradictions are interpreted in terms of a shift in the class struggle to the international arena:

> While one end of the class struggle is being conducted within the boundaries of the USSR, its other end stretches

[2] The first "authentic" formulation in Stalin's "Results of the Work of the Fourteenth Party Conference" (written in 1925). See *Sochineniia* (Works) (13 vols.; Moscow, Gospolitizdat, 1946-51), VII, 90-132.
[3] Stalin, "Results of the Work of the Fourteenth Party Conference," quoted in his *Problems of Leninism* (New York, International Publishers, 1934), p. 63.
[4] Stalin, "Letter to Ivanov," in *The Strategy and Tactics of World Communism*, House Document No. 619, Supplement I (Washington, D.C., U.S. Government Printing Office, 1948), p. 151.
[5] Rozental, *Marksistskii dialekticheskii metod* (Marxist Dialectical Method), pp. 293 ff.

out to the territories of the bourgeois states surrounding us.
. . . The more acute aspect of class struggle affecting the
USSR has now been transferred to the international
arena.[6]

According to Marx, the class struggle is international by its very nature; it would be meaningless to
talk about a "shift" to the international arena. The
Soviet Marxist notion has a different connotation: it
tries to adjust the Marxian theory of the class struggle
to the historical fact of its "neutralization" in the advanced industrial countries. The notion is linked to
the "two-camp" doctrine; the "democratic socialist"
camp, led by the Soviet Union, represents the fight for
the "real" class interests of the international proletariat.
Since the Western proletariat is geographically "enclosed" in the "imperialist camp" (although "in reality" belonging to the socialist camp), it cannot effectively assert its "real" interest—this function rather
devolves upon the group of nations joined in the Soviet
camp. The conflict between the real and the immediate
interests of the proletariat, contained from the beginning in Marxian theory, now becomes the conflict
between two international groupings: the "external"
proletariat of the backward countries is supposed to
fight for the real interest, assuming the historical task
of the proletariat as a whole. With this change in
protagonist, the content and strategy of the class
struggle also change. The class struggle becomes a
fight for space and populations, and the social issues
become a function of political issues. The class interests
of the Western proletariat (and for that matter of the
entire proletariat) are sustained in Soviet policy only

[6] Stalin in 1937, quoted in a lecture on the "Marxist-Leninist
Theory of Classes and Class Struggle," Soviet Home Service,
Moscow Radio, March 5, 1951. See also Rozental, *Marksistskii
dialekticheskii metod* (Marxist Dialectical Method), p. 302.

the degree to which they do not conflict with the
political interests of the USSR. Thus, the class struggle
not transferred to the international level, but rather
transubstantiated into an international political struggle.

The transubstantiation of the class struggle vitiates
all attempts to solve the internal contradictions of
Soviet society without changing its very structure.
Marxism depends, for the attainment of its goals, on
the solution of the conflict between the productive
forces and their repressive organization and utilization. According to Marx, the abolition of capitalism is
not an end in itself but the means for solving this
conflict, thereby terminating the enslavement of man
by his labor and the domination of men by men. And
in so far as such enslavement is institutionalized in
the process of production, it can be abolished only in
the process of production, and the individuals can be
free only if they themselves control production. There
may be several stages on this way to freedom—even
stages of repression (Marx has sketched them in his
Critique of the Gotha Program)—but unless this way
is traveled by the laboring class itself, as the sole
historical agent of liberation, the socialist revolution
has no *raison d'être*. And if the revolution does not
from the beginning reverse the relationship between
the laborer and the means of his labor, that is to say,
transfer control over them to him, it does not have a
raison d'être essentially different from that of capitalist
society. Abolition of private property in the means of
production is thus substantially linked with transfer
of control to the laborers themselves. As long as such
transfer is not accomplished, the revolution is bound
to reproduce the very antagonisms which it strives to
overcome. They appear in manifold forms: as the

repressive utilization of the nationalized means c
production, as the contrast between the level of pro
ductivity and the level of consumption, as the confli
between social and individual needs, between stat
and private and semiprivate property; or in the inter
national arena, between the interests of the USSI
and those of the foreign Communist parties, betwee
the objectives of national Soviet security and those c
socialist policy. They persist even if "socialism in on
country" becomes so to speak "socialism in one orbit,
for, in the last analysis, they are due to the very factor
which brought about and sustained the coexistence c
the two systems. If Soviet Marxism justifies the per
petuation of the repressive state machine by th
continued prevalence of the "capitalist threat," it ac
mits that the structure of Soviet society still is ar
tagonistic; and that the solution of these antagonism
depends on a fundamental change in the internationa
constellation. In 1938, Stalin implied that the interna
contradictions had been solved by the successfu
building of socialism in the USSR;[7] in 1952, he em
phasized again the internal contradictions, which no
reappear on a different level.[8]

The historical situation thus overrides the Stalinis
conception of "socialism in one country," according t
which the internal contradictions could be solved b
the Soviet state while the external contradictions con
tinued to prevail. The external contradictions per
petuate the internal contradictions. According to Sovie
Marxism, the "capitalist environment" enforces th

[7] "Letter to Ivanov," in *The Strategy and Tactics of Worl
Communism*, House Document 619, Supplement I, p. 150.
[8] "Economic Problems of Socialism," in *Current Sovie
Policies*, ed. by Leo Gruliow (New York, F. A. Praeger, 1953)
pp. 5, 11, 14. See below, pp. 151 f.

ontinued strengthening of the repressive political and
military establishment and prevents the free utilization
f the productive forces for the satisfaction of individ-
al needs. But the continued strengthening of the
oviet political and military establishment in turn
erpetuates the "capitalist environment" and even
romotes its intercontinental unification. Ever since
.enin, Soviet Marxism has held that the USSR will
ltimately not be able to survive unless it succeeds in
reaking the deadlock in its own favor. The break is
xpected to come about through the reactivation of
ne "inherent capitalist contradictions" in the "im-
erialist camp." They are frozen in the Western
efense economy; the dissolution of this integrated
olitical economy is, therefore, the indispensable first
bjective.

But the Soviet leadership can hope to attain this
bjective only if the USSR is no longer a military and
olitical threat to the West, that is, if the productive
ower of the Soviet state is redirected to serve the
eeds and faculties of its citizens. This would mean
hat production and the production relations are re-
rganized in such a way that the rise of the level of
naterial and intellectual culture is not the mere by-
roduct but the goal of the social effort. To Soviet
Marxism, such a transformation of Soviet society ap-
ears as a historical necessity, as a requirement of
nternational politics in the era of coexistence. Soviet
Marxism is forced to recognize the interdependence
f the two sets of contradictions which makes the
ocial issues determine the political issues. The vital
im of breaking the deadlock can be achieved only
y a transformation of Soviet society which is to estab-
ish the economic and cultural superiority of socialism

over capitalism, to spread socialism "by contagion,"
and thus to provide the basis for unfreezing the class
struggle in the capitalist world.

In order to evaluate the prospects of this transformation, we shall have to discuss the social structure
of the Soviet state, which, according to Soviet theory
is to remain the "directing agent" of social change.

5

THE DIALECTIC OF
THE SOVIET STATE

A brief summary suffices to recall the chief elements
in Stalin's theory of the retention and growth of the
socialist state. In contrast to Engels's formula of the
"withering away" of the state, which is valid for the
victory of socialism in all or in a majority of countries,
the socialist state must assume new decisive functions
under the conditions of "socialism in one country" and
"capitalist encirclement." These functions change in
accordance with the internal development and the
international situation. In the first phase of the development (from the October Revolution to the "elimination of the exploiting classes"), the functions of the
state were: (*a*) "to suppress the overthrown classes
inside the country," (*b*) "to defend the country from
foreign attack," and (*c*) "economic organization and
cultural education." In the second phase (from the
"elimination of the capitalist elements in town and
country" to the "complete victory of the socialist system and the adoption of the new constitution") function (*a*) ceased and was supplanted by that of "pro-
tecting socialist property"; functions (*b*) and (*c*)
"fully remained." Moreover, the state is to continue

also in the period of communism "unless the capitalist encirclement" is liquidated, and "unless the danger of foreign military attack has disappeared"—only then will it "atrophy."[1] As early as 1930, Stalin had condensed the dialectic of the socialist state to the formula: "The highest possible development of the power of the State with the object of preparing the conditions for the dying away of the State—that is the Marxist formula."[2] Later on, emphasis was placed on the strengthening of the state power prior to and during the transition to communism.[3]

The continuation of the state in the first period of socialism is implied in the original Marxian conception. Marx assumed that the "enslaving subordination of the individuals to the division of labor" would continue during the First Phase of socialism.[4] Consequently, the state would continue; its "withering away would be gradual and preceded by a period of transformation" of the political institutions. Thus was the development outlined by Engels as early as 1847, and it was again emphasized in the eighties in his polemic against the anarchists:

The anarchists . . . declare that the proletarian revolution must begin with the abolition of the political organization of the state. But the only organization which the proletariat finds available (*fertig*) after its victory is the

[1] Stalin, "Report on the Work of the Central Committee to the Eighteenth Party Congress," in *Leninism* (New York, International Publishers, 1942), p. 474.
[2] Stalin, *Political Report to the Sixteenth Party Congress* (New York, Workers Library Publishers, 1930), p. 171.
[3] Stalin, *Marksizm i voprosy iazykoznaniia* (Marxism and Linguistic Problems) (Moscow, Gospolitizdat, 1950). See also M. M. Rozental, *Marksistskii dialekticheskii metod* (Marxist Dialectical Method) (Moscow, Gospolitizdat, 1951), p. 109.
[4] "Critique of the Gotha Program," in Marx and Engels *Selected Works* (2 vols.; Moscow, Foreign Languages Publishing House, 1949-50), II, 23; see above, p. 6.
[5] *Principles of Communism*, Questions 17 and 18.

state. This state may have to undergo considerable changes before it can fulfil its new functions. But to destroy it in one moment would mean to destroy the only organization with which the victorious proletariat would exercise the power which it has just conquered—to subdue its capitalist enemies and to carry through that economic revolution of society without which the victory would of necessity end in a new defeat.[6]

The Marx quotations around which Lenin built his refutation of Kautsky in *State and Revolution* do not contradict this conception.[7] The "state machinery" which is to be shattered, the "bureaucratic and military machinery" which cannot be transferred from one hand to the other but must be "broken up," is the machinery of the bourgeois class state. To be sure, according to Marx, all historical forms of the state were forms of the class state—but in so far as the first phase of socialism still is "affected" with its capitalist heritage, so is its state. However, while the socialist state continues to exercise coercive functions, its substance has undergone a fundamental change: the socialist state *is* the proletariat, constituted as the ruling class.[8] Consequently, in terms of class position

[6] Letter to Ph. van Patten, April 18, 1883, in Marx and Engels, *Briefe an A. Bebel, W. Liebknecht, K. Kautsky und Andere* (Moscow, Verlagsgenossenschaft Ausländischer Arbeiter in der USSR, 1933), I, 296. Engels's statement in "Anti-Dühring," written only five years earlier, seems to contradict this notion. There he says that the "first act in which the state appears really as the representative of the whole society—the appropriation of the means of production in the name of the society—is at the same time its last independent act as a state." However, the qualifying terms ("really," "the whole of society," "independent") would make it possible to locate this "act" at the end rather than the beginning of the first phase.

[7] *State and Revolution* (New York, International Publishers, 1932), pp. 25, 33.

[8] "Communist Manifesto," in *The Strategy and Tactics of World Communism*, House Document No. 619, Supplement I (Washington, D.C., U.S. Government Printing Office, 1948), p. 19.

and class interests, the subject and the object of coercion are identical.[9] In this sense, the state of the first
phase is a "non-state," the state "broken up" and
"shattered." [1] Since political power is, "properly" speaking, "merely the organized power of one class for
oppressing another," [2] the class identity between the
subject and object of the state now tends to transform
coercion into rational administration. Marx and Engels
summarized the changes in the function of the state
as this very transformation: "The public functions will
lose their political character and be transformed into
the simple administrative function of watching over
the true interest of society." [3]

In contrast to this conception, the Soviet state exercises throughout political and governmental functions
against the proletariat itself; domination remains a
specialized function in the division of labor and is
as such the monopoly of a political, economic, and
military bureaucracy. This function is perpetuated by
the centralized authoritarian organization of the productive process, directed by groups which determine

[9] Except, of course, where the state power is directed against
the "capitalist enemies" within and without. But in the
Marxian conception, this function does not change the basic
structure of the socialist state; military and police actions
against the class enemy are seen as a *levée en masse*, as actions
of the armed people themselves.
[1] Marx, Letter to Kugelmann, April 12, 1871, in Marx and
Engels, *Selected Works*, II, 420. See Lenin, *State and Revolution*, p. 33.
[2] "Communist Manifesto," in *The Strategy and Tactics of
World Communism*, House Document No. 619, Supplement I,
p. 19.
[3] Engels, "On Authority," in Marx and Engels, *Selected
Works*, I, 577. See also Engels's famous formulation in "Anti-
Dühring": "The functions of government transform themselves
into simple functions of administration." See Marx and Engels,
*Die Allianz der sozialistischen Demokratie und die Interna-
tionale Arbeiterassoziation*, ed. by Wilhelm Blos under the title
Marx oder Bakunin? (Stuttgart, Volksverlag für Wirtschaft und
Verkehr, 1920), p. 14.

the needs of society (the social product and its distribution) independent of the collective control of the ruled population. Whether or not these groups constitute a "class" in the Marxian sense is a problem of Marxist exegesis.[4] The fact is that Soviet Marxism itself stresses the "directing" function of the state as distinguished from the underlying institutions, and that this state retains the separation of the "immediate producers" from collective control over the process of production. Soviet Marxism justifies this "anomaly" by the anomalous circumstances of socialism in a "capitalist environment." These circumstances are supposed to require the continuation and even the growth of the state as a system of *political* institutions, and the exercise by the state of oppressive economic, military, police, and educational functions over and against society. The Soviet state thus takes shape exactly as that structure which Engels described as characteristic of class society: the "common societal functions" become a "new branch of the division of labor" and thereby constitute *particular* interests separate from those of the population.[5] The state is again a reified, hypostatized power.

As such a power, the state, according to Soviet

[4] Clearly, if "class" is defined in terms of the relation to the basic means of production, and the latter in terms of ownership, the Soviet bureaucracy is *not* a class. If *control* over the means of production is made the criterion, the question whether or not such control is delegated and in turn effectively controlled by the "immediate producers" would be decisive. We use "class" here as designating a group which exercises governmental (including managerial) functions as a "separate" function in the social division of labor—with or without special privileges. Thus, if the bureaucracy would be open to ascent "from below," it would still be a class as long as the separateness of its function makes it independent from the people whom it manages and administers.

[5] Engels, Letter to Conrad Schmidt, October 27, 1890, in *Über Historischen* Materialismus, ed. by Hermann Duncker (Berlin, Internationaler Arbeiterverlag, 1930), II, 140.

Marxism, becomes the Archimedean point from which
the world is moved into socialism, the "basic instrument" for the establishment of socialism and communism. Soviet Marxism links the perpetuated hypostatization of the state to the very progress of socialist
construction.[6] The argument runs as follows: With the
overthrow of capitalism and the nationalization of the
economy, the Bolshevik Revolution laid the foundation
for a state which represents the interests of the urban
and rural proletariat. The state is their state, and,
consequently, the further development of the revolution takes place "from above" rather than "from below." The liquidation of the "old bourgeois economic
order in rural areas" and the creation of a "socialist
collective farm order" was such a revolution from
above, "on the initiative of the existing regime with
the support of the basic masses of the peasantry." [7]
The firm institutionalization of the state in the revolution from above took shape under the first Five-Year
Plan, which revolutionized the economic order of the
country not only over and above and against the
"immediate interests" of workers and peasants, but also
by subjecting them to the bureaucratic-authoritarian
organization of production. According to Stalinism,
transition to the subsequent stages of socialism will
likewise be made by strengthening the institutionalized
state rather than by dissolving it.[8] But the hypostatization of the regime implied in these formulations
might boomerang against alterations in the political

    [6] Ts. A. Stepanian, "Usloviia i puti perekhoda ot sotsializma
k kommunizmu" (The Conditions and the Paths of the Transition from Socialism to Communism), in *O sovetskom sotsialisticheskom obshchestve* (On Soviet Socialist Society), ed. by F.
Konstantinov (Moscow, Gospolitizdat, 1948), p. 544.
    [7] Stalin, *Marksizm i voprosy iazykoznaniia* (Marxism and
Linguistic Problems) (Moscow, Gospolitizdat, 1950).
    [8] See below, p. 152.

structure necessitated by international and internal developments. The power of the state has its objective limits. In the later period of Stalinism, Soviet Marxism emphasized that the state itself is subject to general socioeconomic laws, that its forms "are changing and will continue to change in line with the development of our country and with the changes in the international situation." [9] In Soviet Marxist evaluation, such internal and international developments were asserting themselves on the ground of the achievements of Stalinism and were calling for a corresponding change in Soviet theory and strategy.

Before outlining the trend in the development of the state envisaged by Soviet Marxism, the question must be asked: Who or what is that Soviet state? Neither the rise of the Soviet intelligentsia as a new ruling group, nor its composition and its privileges are any longer disputed facts—least so in the USSR. The recruitment and training of highly qualified specialists, technicians, managers, etc., is continually emphasized and their privileges are advertised.[1] Moreover the uninterrupted growth of this group is considered one of the essential preconditions for the transition to communism.[2] Decisive in the problem of the development of the state are not merely the privileges of the governmental bureaucracy, its numerical strength, and its caste character, but the basis and scope of its power. Obviously the bureauc-

---

[9] Stalin, "Report on the Work of the Central Committee to the Eighteenth Party Congress," in *Leninism* (New York, International Publishers, 1942), p. 473.

[1] At least since 1935. See Stalin's speech to the graduates of the Red Army Academy in *Leninism*, pp. 363 f.

[2] For example see Stepanian, "Usloviia i puti perekhoda ot sotsializma k kommunizmu" (The Conditions and the Paths of the Transition from Socialism to Communism), in *O sovetskom sotsialisticheskom obshchestve* (On Soviet Socialist Society), pp. 516 f. and 520.

racy has a vital interest in maintaining and enhancing its privileged position. Obviously, there are conflicts among various groups within the bureaucracy. In order to evaluate their significance for the tendential development of Soviet society, an attempt must be made to determine whether or not there is a political and economic basis for using the special position of the bureaucracy (or special positions within the bureaucracy) for exploding and changing the structure of Soviet society. The following paragraphs suggest only some of the general aspects pertaining to such an attempt.

We have emphasized that Soviet Marxism admits the existence of contradictory interests in Soviet society[3] and derives them from the existence of different forms of Socialist property and labor. As specific sources of contradictions are mentioned: the coexistence of state, collective, and private property in the means of production; the difference between mental and physical labor; the stratification into intelligentsia, workers, and peasants; the uneven development of the two main divisions of social production. As long as the bureaucracy is a special branch in the division of labor, engendering a special position in society,

[3] "Socialism in our country has been built upon the basis of the solution of internal contradictions by our own forces." *Bol'shaia Sovetskaia Entsiklopediia* (Large Soviet Encyclopedia) (65 vols.; Moscow, OGIZ RSFSR, 1926-47), XLVII, col. 378. For the enumeration of specific contradictions, see, for example, Stalin's speech to the Stakhanovites, 1935, in *Leninism*, p. 368, and his "Economic Problems of Socialism in the USSR," in *Current Soviet Policies*, ed. by Leo Gruliow (New York, F. A. Praeger, 1953), *passim;* Rozental, *Marksistskii dialekticheskii metod* (Marxist Dialectical Method), pp. 283-88; Stepanian, "Usloviia i puti perekhoda ot sotsializma k kommunizmu" (The Conditions and the Paths of the Transition from Socialism to Communism), in *O sovetskom sotsialisticheskom obshchestve* (On Soviet Socialist Society), pp. 528-31; and *Pravda*, August 20, 1947.

it has a separate, special interest. According to Soviet Marxism, these "internal" contradictions, and with them the separate position of the bureaucracy, will "flatten out" with the gradual equalization of mental and physical labor, which in turn will result from the gradual elimination of the lag of production relations behind the growth of the productive forces. The elimination of the class position of the bureaucracy (but not of the bureaucracy itself) thus will appear as a "by-product" of the transition from socialism to communism. At that stage, the bureaucracy would still exercise special functions but no longer within an institutionalized, hierarchical division of functions; the bureaucracy would be "open" and lose its "political" content to the degree to which, with the wealth of the material and intellectual productive forces, the general societal functions would become exchangeable among the individuals. Is the Soviet Marxist assumption of such a trend even theoretically consistent with the actual structure of the Soviet state?

Bureaucracy by itself, no matter how huge it is, does not generate self-perpetuating power unless it has an economic base of its own from which its position is derived, or unless it is allied with other social groups which possess such a power base. Naturally, the traditional sources of economic power are not available to the Soviet bureaucracy; it does not own the nationalized means of production. But obviously "the people," who constitutionally own the means of production, do not control them. Control, therefore, and not ownership must be the decisive factor. But unless further defined, "control" is an insufficient index for the real locus of power. Is it exercised simply by particular interests independent enough to assert themselves against others, or are

these interests themselves subject to overriding laws
and forces? With respect to the Soviet system and its
organization of production, distinction must be made
between technical-administrative and social control.
The two levels of control would coincide if those
which manage the industrial and agricultural key
establishments determine by and for themselves and
as a special group entrepreneurial and labor policies,
thereby wielding decisive influence over the social
need and its satisfaction. Such a coincidence cannot
be taken for granted. In Soviet doctrine, it is the
Party which exercises the social control overriding
all technical-administrative control, and since the
Party is fused with the state, social control assumes
the form of centralized and planned political control.
But the same question as to the ultimate superseding
control must be asked with respect to the Party—even
its top leadership comprises various groups and
interests, including managerial ones. Obviously, the
"people" can be excluded: there is no effective social
control "from below." Thus, two possibilities are left:
either (1) a specific group within the bureaucracy
exercises control over all the rest of the bureaucracy
(in which case this group would be the autonomous
subject of social control); or (2) the bureaucracy as
a "class" is truly sovereign, i.e., the ruling group (in
which case social and technical-administrative controls would coincide). This alternative will be discussed
presently.

Personal power, even if effectively institutionalized,
does not define social control. Stalin's dictatorship
may well have overridden all divergent interests by
virtue of his factual power. However, this personal
power was itself subject to the requirements of the
social system on whose continued functioning it

depended, and over and above the subsistence minimum, these requirements were codetermined by the interests controlling the industrial and agricultural basis, and by those of the police and the army. The same holds true, to a much greater extent, for the post-Stalinist leadership. The search for the locus of social control thus leads back from personal dictatorship to the alternative formulated above. But there seems to be no separate homogeneous group to which social control could be meaningfully attributed. The top ruling group is itself changing and comprises "representatives" of various bureaucracies and branches of the bureaucracies, economic as well as political: management, army, party. Each of them has a special interest and aspires for social control. But the monopolization of power is counteracted by two forces: on the one side, the Central Plan, in spite of its vagaries, loopholes, and corrections, ultimately supersedes and integrates the special interests; on the other side, the entire bureaucracy, up to the highest level, is subject to the competitive terror, or, after the relaxation of the terror, to the highly incalculable application of political or punitive measures, leading to the loss of power. To be sure, the Central Plan is itself the work of the bureaucracy in the main branches of the system: government, party, armed forces, management; but it is the result of their combined and adjusted interests and negotiations, ensuing in a sort of general interest which in turn depends on the internal growth of Soviet society. This relation also played an important role in the development of the terror.

Terror is the centralized, methodical application of incalculable violence (incalculable for the objects of the terror, and also for the top groups and even

the practitioners of the terror)—not only in an emergency situation, but in a normal state of affairs.
As long as the Soviet state relied on such incalculable
application, it relied on terroristic force—although the
terror would approximate a normal competitive social
system to the degree to which the punitive measures
(such as removal from office, demotion) would be
nonviolent. In its historical function, terror may be
progressive or regressive,[4] depending upon whether
it actually promotes, through the destruction of repressive institutions, the growth of liberal ones, and the
rational utilization of the productive forces. In the
Soviet state, the terror is of a twofold nature: technological and political. Inefficiency and poor performance at the technical and business level are
punished; so is any kind of nonconformity: politically
and dangerously suspect attitudes, opinions, behavior.
The two forms are interconnected, and efficiency is
certainly often judged on political grounds. However,
with the elimination of all organized opposition, and
with the continued success of the totalitarian administration, the terror tends to become predominantly
technological, and, in the USSR itself, strictly political
terror seems to be the exception rather than the rule.
The completely standardized clichés of the political
charges, which no longer even pretend to be rational,
plausible, and consistent, may well serve to conceal
the real reason for the indictment: differences in the
timing and implementation of administrative measures
on whose substance the conflicting parties agree.

The technological terror is omnipresent—but this
very omnipresence implies a high degree of indiffer-

---

[4] See Franz Neumann, "Notes on the Theory of Dictatorship,"
in *The Democratic and the Authoritarian State* (Glencoe, Ill.,
Free Press, 1957), pp. 233-56.

ence toward special privilege and position. An action
started on a low level may involve the highest level
if the circumstances are "favorable." The chiefs themselves are not immune—they are not the absolute
masters of oppression. The circumstances which set
the machine in motion against a specific target seem
to be the end-constellation of numerous cross currents
in the areas of the respective bureaucracies. The
ultimate decision in prominent cases is also likely to
be the result of negotiations and compromises among
the top groups—each representing its own "apparatus,"
but each apparatus again subject to competitive
controls within the framework of the Central Plan
and the then prevailing principles of foreign and
domestic policy. This framework leaves much room
for personal and clique influences and interests, corruption, and profiteering; it also permits one group
(and one individual of the group) to come out on
top—but it also sets the limits beyond which the
monopolization of power cannot go without upsetting
the structure on which Soviet power rests.

These limits are circumscribed by the exigencies
of the planned growth and correlation of the economic, political, and military establishments. The
rate and mode of growth, and the priorities of and
within the main establishments are apparently determined through struggles and compromises between
competing vested interests. Sooner or later, however,
the outcome must conform to the basic trend of
the construction of Soviet society and to the principles
which have governed this trend since the first Five-
Year Plan. Once institutionalized, they have their
own momentum and their own objective requirements;
the vested interests themselves depend on the observ-
ance of these requirements. The principles are altered

and adjusted in accordance with the changing domestic and international situation, but a long-range general trend emerges into which the modifications are integrated. When Stepanian stated that the development of Marxism presupposes "the unchangeability of its principles and foundations,"[5] this was more than propaganda: identical principles (Marxist or not) have indeed governed the controls in all basic spheres of the Soviet system. They are likely to reassert themselves in the conflict of competing powers and vested interests because they pertain to the very structure of the society in which these powers and interests prevail. For example, the efforts to reduce the investments in heavy industry in favor of light industry and an increase in consumers' goods, which came into the open after Stalin's death, assumed the form of a struggle for power among certain groups of the top leadership. However, the long-range trend of Soviet industrialization and the political setup defined by it seem to have predetermined the decision to a great extent. The Stalinist construction of Soviet society rested on the sustained priority of heavy industry; a fundamental shift in the balance would mean a fundamental shift in the structure itself—in the economic as well as political system. Such a shift was not precluded by the Stalinist program—on the contrary: we emphasized the "tentative" character of this program and its orientation on a "second phase." However, this change is not within the discretion and power of any particular group or individual: it depends on the international constellation and on the economic and political level of the productive forces

[5] "Usloviia i puti perekhoda ot sotsializma k kommunizmu" (The Conditions and the Paths of Transition from Socialism to Communism), in *O sovetskom sotsialisticheskom obshchestve* (On Soviet Socialist Society), p. 482.

of Soviet society. More specifically, it depends on the attainment of the capacity level of the advanced industrial countries and the corresponding relative weakening of the capitalist world. Whether or not this level has been attained, and whether or not the international situation is feasible for the change, is a political decision, to be fought out among the leadership of the top bureaucracies—but the decision will be cancelled if it is not corroborated and "verified" by the objective factors of the international and domestic situation, that is, in the last analysis, by the international effectiveness of Soviet policy.

Another example for the perseverance of basic objectives and principles overriding the bureaucratic "struggle for power" may be provided by the agricultural policy: it aims, through all turns, regressions, leaps, and corrections and through consecutive stages of collectivization, at the establishment of complete socialist property on the land, total mechanization, and assimilation of urban and rural life and labor. In foreign policy, through "hard" and "soft" periods, through local wars and "peace offensives," Lenin's guidance stands supreme: to preserve the "respite" for the building of socialism and communism in coexistence with the capitalist world. Here, too, the interpretation of the governing principles, and the decision on the timing and scope of the measures which they stipulate, remain ultimately the monopoly of a top group of leaders. But no matter how its composition and number may change, nor how the extent of consultation and compromise with the lower strata of the bureaucracy may vary, the governing principles seem to be rigid enough to define the limits of special powers and to preclude their institutionalization within a system governed by these principles.

The Soviet bureaucracy thus does not seem to possess a basis for the effective perpetuation of special interests against the overriding general requirements of the social system on which it lives. The bureaucracy constitutes a separate class which controls the underlying population through control of the economic, political, and military establishments, and exercise of this control engenders a variety of special interests which assert themselves in the control; however, they must compromise and ultimately succumb to the general policy which none of the special interests can change by virtue of its special power. Does this mean that the bureaucracy represents the common interest of society as a whole?

In a society composed of competing groups with different economic, occupational, and administrative interests, "common interest" is not per se a meaningful term. Even if one assumes that the general rise in the material and cultural living conditions with a maximum of individual liberty and security defines the common interest of every civilized society, it appears that in any nonhomogeneous society the realization of this interest will proceed in conflict with the interests of some of the (privileged) groups in society. The common interest would not be identical with the interest of all and each; it would remain an "ideological" concept. This antagonistic situation prevails not only in the relationship between the bureaucracy and the underlying population, but also in that between the urban and rural groups, and even between different subgroups within these groups, such as between male and female, skilled and unskilled workers. Even in a highly advanced industrial society with abundant resources, the rise in the general standard of living and of general freedom could take place only as a most unequal development, overriding the immediate interests of large parts of the population. Just as the social need is not identical with the individual needs, so is the realization of "universal" liberty and justice at one and the same time also injustice and unfreedom in individual cases (and even in the case of whole social groups). The very universality of right and law—the guarantor of freedom and justice—demands such negation and limitation by virtue of the fact that it must necessarily abstract from "particularities."

The inequality implied in the common interest would be much greater in a backward society; neither nationalization nor central planning per se would eliminate it. The common interest would retain a high degree of "abstractness" as against the immediate interest (although this abstractness may be gradually reduced as society develops). In other words, the traditional distinction between the general (common) interest and the sum-total of particular interests would hold true, and the former would have to be defined in terms of its own—as a separate entity, as the social interest over and above individual interests. Soviet Marxism defines the former in relation to the productive forces and their organization; the social interest is said to be represented by those groups and interests which promote the development of the productive forces. This relation is itself a historical factor, to be defined in terms of the political and economic situation of the respective society.

In the case of Soviet society the accelerated development of its productive forces is considered a prerequisite for the survival and competitive strength of the Soviet state in the circumstances of "coexistence." The position of the bureaucracy thus depends on the expansion of the productive apparatus, and the specific and conflicting interests within the bureaucracy are superseded, through the mechanisms of technology and force, diplomacy and power politics, by this common social interest. The Soviet bureaucracy therefore represents the social interest in a hypostatized form, in which the individual interests are separated from the individuals and arrogated by the state.

The Soviet state emerges as the institutionalized collective in which the Marxian distinction between the immediate and the real (objective historical) interest is made the rationale for the building of the political structure. The state is the manifestation of the real (the social) interest, but as such the state is "not yet" identical with the interests of the people whom it rules: their immediate interests do "not yet" coincide with the objective social interest. For example, the people want less work, more freedom, more consumer goods—but, according to the official theory, the still prevailing backwardness and scarcity necessitate the continued subordination of these interests to the social interest of armament and industrialization. This is the old discrepancy between the individual and society, represented by the state; however, in Soviet theory, it occurs at a new stage of the historical process. Formerly, the state represented not the interest of society as a whole but that of the ruling class. To be sure, in a sense, the class state too represented the collective interest[6] in so far as it organized and sustained the orderly reproduction of society as a whole and the development of the productive forces. However, the conflict between their rational development in the common interest and

[6] See below, p. 105.

their private-profit utilization was, within the framework of the class state, insoluble and vitiated the identity of interests. As this conflict ripened, the class state would become of necessity ever more regressive and a fetter to the development of society. In contrast, the Soviet state is supposed to run the opposite course, capable of resolving the conflict[7] and of establishing the harmony between individual and social need on the basis of an all-out development of productivity.

[7] See above, pp. 78 f., and below, p. 152.

6

BASE AND
SUPERSTRUCTURE—
REALITY AND IDEOLOGY

In Marxian theory, the state belongs to the super-structure inasmuch as it is *not* simply the direct political expression of the basic relationships of production but contains elements which, as it were, "compensate" for the class relationships of production. The state, being and remaining the state of the ruling class, sustains *universal* law and order and thereby guarantees at least a modicum of equality and security for the whole of society. Only by virtue of these elements can the class state fulfill the function of "moderating" and keeping within the bounds of "order" the class conflicts generated by the production relations.[1] It is this "mediation" which gives the state the appearance of a universal interest over and above the conflicting particular interests. The universal function of the state is itself determined by the

[1] Engels, *Origin of the Family, Private Property, and the State* (New York, International Publishers, 1942), p. 155. See also Marx and Engels, *The German Ideology* (New York, International Publishers, 1939), pp. 40-41.

base, but contains factors transcending and even
antagonistic to the base—factors which may become
semi-independent forces, in turn actively affecting
the base in various ways.

Engels distinguished two principal modes in which
the state can "react" on the basic economic process,
namely, either counter to or "in the same direction"
as the economic development. In the latter case, the
state "accelerates" the economic development.[2] The
second mode of reaction presupposes conformity
between the political superstructure and the development of the productive forces—a conformity which
Marxian theory denies for all but the ascending
phases of capitalist society (and class society in
general). According to Soviet Marxism, the Bolshevik
Revolution brought the political superstructure "into
agreement" with the economic base, while the nationalization of the means of production rendered possible
centralized control over the economic development.
The economic laws continue to operate as objective
forces determining the superstructure, they can neither be "created" nor "changed" by the state, but
they have become susceptible to conscious use and
application.[3] This, according to Soviet Marxist theory,
is the decisive difference between the Soviet and the
capitalist superstructure. Both forms of the state
constitute a "political superstructure," that is to say,
they are determined by the respective "economic
structure" of society, but while this determination is

[2] Letter to Conrad Schmidt, October 27, 1890, in Marx and
Engels, Selected Works (2 vols.; Moscow, Foreign Languages
Publishing House, 1949-50), II, 447.
[3] Stalin, "Economic Problems of Socialism in the USSR," in
Current Soviet Policies, ed. by Leo Gruliow (New York, F. A.
Praeger, 1953), p. 18. See also articles from Izvestiia, January
23, 1953, in Current Digest of the Soviet Press, VI, No. 1
(February 14, 1953), 3-6; and below, pp. 151 f.

blind and supreme in the capitalist state, the Soviet state can "direct" and "control" it. Thus, whereas under capitalism "it is rather the state that is controlled by the capitalist economy," the Soviet state "becomes the directing force of the country's economic development," the "directing force" of the economy.[4]

Some analysts of Soviet developments have seen in this redefinition of the relation between base and superstructure (which is generalized and authenticated in Stalin's *Marxism and Linguistic Problems*) a revision of the fundamental Marxian conception.[5] In reality, it is only an application of Engels's proposition concerning the reciprocal action (*Wechselwirkung*) between base and superstructure. The state, if it "accelerates" the economic development, "becomes a very great active force, helping (cooperating) with its base to form and consolidate itself; it takes all measures to help the new order to destroy and liquidate the old basis and the old classes."[6] This statement from Stalin's *Marxism and Linguistic Problems* refers not only to the state but to the superstructure in general. These formulations follow logi-

---

[4] G. Glezermann, "The Socialist State—Mighty Instrumentality for Building Communism," in *Current Digest of the Soviet Press*, IV, No. 41 (November 24, 1951), 7-10 (translated from *Izvestiia*, October 12, 1951). This does not preclude that "the bourgeois state influences the economic development." Stalin expands on this formulation in his "Economic Problems of Socialism," in *Current Soviet Policies*, pp. 1-20. See below, pp. 152 f.

[5] Robert Daniels, "State and Revolution: A Case Study in the Genesis and Transformation of Communist Ideology," *American Slavic and East European Review*, XII, No. 1 (February, 1953), 22-43.

[6] For the Soviet Marxist evaluation of Stalin's statement, see M. B. Mittin, *Novyi vydaiushchiiisia vklad I. V. Stalina v razvitie marksistsko-leninskoi teorii* (The Distinguished New Contribution of J. V. Stalin to the Development of Marxist-Leninist Theory) (Moscow, Vsesoiuznoe obshchestvo po rasprostraneniiu politicheskikh i nauchnykh znanii, 1950), especially p. 13.

cally from the assumption, indisputable for Soviet
Marxism, that the Soviet society is a socialist society.
Naturally, a socialist state will have an essentially
different relation to the base than a capitalist state
(in Soviet Marxist language, a nonantagonistic relation). Consequently, the development from socialism
toward communism can equally logically be envisaged
as a nonantagonistic development in the sense that
progress to the "higher stage" does not involve
"destructive" alterations in the base but rather the
gradual unfolding of its potentialities. The existence
of a socialist base would indeed change the entire
traditional function of the superstructure and establish a new relation between ideology and reality.

If we apply the traditional Marxian conception
schematically to Soviet society, the base consists of
the prevailing "productive forces" in the prevailing
production relations.[7] The "producers" are wage earn-
ers and salaried employees of the state, and members
of the collective farms. In the property relation of
the producers to the basic means of production, there
are no class distinctions between the groups making
up Soviet society (intelligentsia, workers, peasants)—
although, of course, vast distinctions exist in terms of
control and living conditions. The superstructure

[7] The controversy as to whether or not Stalin's definition
in *Marxism and Linguistic Problems* excludes the productive
forces from the base is without relevance here. In Marxian
theory, the productive forces constitute per se a more fundamental level than the production relations although they
operate only within specific production relations. For the
whole controversy see the report on the Conference of the
Communist Academy of Social Sciences, February 25 to
March 1, 1952, "Nauchnaia sessiia, posviashchennaia trudam
I. V. Stalina i ika znacheniiu v razvitii obshchestvennykh
nauk" (Scientific Session Devoted to the Works of J. V.
Stalin and to Their Significance in the Development of the
Social Sciences), *Voprosy Filosofii* (Problems of Philosophy)
1952, No. 3, pp. 240-61.

consists of the system of administrative, legal, and cultural institutions, and of the official ideology promulgated by them and transmitted to the various fields of private and public life. As in the classical Marxian scheme, the base determines the superstructure, that is, the latter is shaped by the requirements of the productive apparatus. But the apparatus is nationalized, and these requirements are centrally planned and controlled. This introduces significant changes into the traditional scheme: the state becomes, without intermediary factors, the direct political organization of the productive apparatus, the general manager of the nationalized economy, and the hypostatized collective interest. The functional differences between base and superstructure therefore tend to be obliterated: the latter is methodically and systematically assimilated with the base by depriving the superstructure of those functions which are transcendent and antagonistic to the base. This process, which establishes new foundations for social control, alters the very substance of ideology. The tension between idea and reality, between culture and civilization, between intellectual and material culture—a tension which was one of the driving forces behind Western civilization—is not solved but methodically reduced.

For Marx and Engels, ideology is an illusion (*Schein*), but a necessary illusion, arising from a social organization of production which appears to man as a system of independent, objective laws and forces. As a "reflection" of the actual social basis, the ideology partakes of the truth, but the latter is expressed in false form. The ideas of the ruling class become the ruling ideas and claim universal validity, but the claim is founded on "false consciousness"—

false because the real connection of the ideas with their economic basis and therefore their actual limitations and negations do not enter consciousness.[8] A specific historical content appears as universally valid and serves to provide a prop for a specific social system. However, the function of ideology goes far beyond such service. Into the ideology has entered material which—transmitted from generation to generation—contains the perpetual hopes, aspirations and sufferings of man, his suppressed potentialities the images of integral justice, happiness, and freedom They find their ideological expressions chiefly in religion, philosophy, and art, but also in the juristic and political concepts of liberty, equality, and security

The Marxian notion of ideology here implies a dynamic which leads to a change in the function and weight of ideology relative to the base. The more the base encroaches upon the ideology, manipulating and coordinating it with the established order, the more the ideological sphere which is remotest from the reality (art, philosophy), precisely because of its remoteness, becomes the last refuge for the opposition to this order. When Marx began to elaborate his theory, he was motivated by the conviction that history had at last reached the stage where Reason and Freedom could be transubstantiated from philosophical ideas into political objectives. Philosophy (which Marx considered as the most advanced ideology) was to find its fulfillment in the action of the proletariat,[9] a fulfillment which was at the same time

---

[8] Engels, Letter to Mehring, July 14, 1893, in Marx and Engels, *Selected Works*, II, 451.

[9] Marx, "Zur Kritik der Hegelschen Rechtsphilosophie Einleitung," in Marx and Engels, *Historisch-Kritische Gesam tausgabe*, ed. by D. Rjazonov (Frankfurt, Marx-Engels Archiv Verlagsgesellschaft, 1927), Div. I, I, Pt. 1, pp. 620 f.

the end, the "loss" of philosophy. The proletariat, which provides the "material weapons" for philosophy, finds in philosophy its "conceptual weapons." Philosophy had elaborated the idea of the liberty and dignity of man, of his inalienable rights, his autonomy, his mastery of his life, his potentialities, and his happiness. While class society had rendered these contents ideological, the action of the proletariat, in abolishing class society, would make them reality.

However, the same development which precluded the socialist revolution in the advanced industrial countries vitiated the Marxian notion of the transition from ideology to reality, from philosophy to revolutionary practice. If the proletariat no longer acts as the revolutionary class representing the "absolute negation" of the established order, it no longer furnishes the "material weapons" for philosophy. The situation thus reverts: repelled by reality, Reason and Freedom become again the concern of philosophy. The "essence of man," his "total liberation" is again "experienced [only] in thought" (*in Gedanken erlebt*).[1] Theory—by virtue of its historical position Marxian theory is in its very substance philosophy— again not only anticipates political practice, runs ahead of it, but also upholds the objectives of liberation in the face of a failing practice. In this function, theory becomes again ideology—not as false consciousness, but as conscious distance and dissociation from, even opposition to, the repressive reality. And by the same token, it becomes a political factor of utmost significance. The struggle on the "ideological front" is, for the Soviet state, a struggle for survival. We have seen[2] how, in this struggle, base and

[1] *Ibid.*
[2] See above, pp. 106 f.

superstructure change their relation. According to Soviet Marxism, whereas formerly progress to higher stages of social development necessitated the revolutionary alteration of the established basis, the Soviet state can achieve the transition on the already existing basis, by planful and "scientific direction." The process eliminates previously dominant ideological elements in so far as even the most blatant contradictions and illusions, even nonsense and falsehood, enter into consciousness and are consciously utilized. But this does not take care of the whole content of ideology. The conflict between the growth of productive forces and the repressive production relations to which the entire population is subjected sustains among the population the need for ideological transcendence beyond the repressive reality. According to Marxian theory, this need will disappear "as soon as it is no longer necessary to represent a particular interest as general or the 'general interest' as ruling." [3] In the Soviet system, the "general interest" is hypostatized in the state—an entity separate from the individual interests. To the extent that the latter are still unfulfilled and repelled by reality, they strive for ideological expression; and their force is the more explosive to the regime the more the new economic basis is propagandized as insuring the total liberation of man under communism. The fight against ideological transcendence thus becomes a life-and-death struggle for the regime. Within the ideological sphere, the center of gravity shifts from philosophy to literature and art. The danger zone of *philosophical* transcendence has been brought under control through the absorption of philosophy into the official theory. Metaphysics,

[3] Marx and Engels, *The German Ideology* (New York, International Publishers, 1939), p. 41.

traditionally the chief refuge for the still unrealized ideas of human freedom and fulfillment, is declared to be totally superseded by dialectical materialism and by the emergence of a rational society in socialism. Ethical philosophy, transformed into a pragmatic system of rules and standards of behavior, has become an integral part of state policy.[4] What remains of these branches of philosophy is their methodical negation. The fight against Western philosophy, "bourgeois objectivism," idealism, and so forth (strikingly exemplified by the Aleksandrov controversy in 1946), aims at discrediting philosophical trends and categories which, by virtue of their transcendence, seemed to endanger the "closed" political and ideological system. (As a theoretical task, the aim seems to be self-defeating in view of the fact that the Marxian conception has cancelled but preserved [*aufgehoben*] the tabooed "bourgeois" elements. It is not surprising, therefore, that the controversy nowhere moves at the level of a substantive critique of "bourgeois philosophy.")[5] With this negation of philosophy,[6] the main ideological struggle then is directed against the transcendence in art. Soviet art must be "realistic."

Realism can be—and has been—a highly critical and progressive form of art; confronting reality "as

[4] The second part of this study will discuss the transformation.

[5] The taboo on philosophy affects even those Marxist contributions which marked a milestone in the development of post-Marxian theory, most notably Georg Lukács's *Geschichte und Klassenbewusstsein* (Berlin, Der Malik-Verlag, 1923), while the same author's *Die Zerstörung der Vernunft* (Berlin, Aufbau-Verlag, 1954) may serve as an example of the deterioration of the Marxist critique.

[6] For the reasons indicated above, a substantive discussion of Soviet philosophy lies outside the scope of this study. The best and most comprehensive survey is in Gustav A. Wetter, *Der dialektische Materialismus; seine Geschichte und sein System in der Soviet-Union* (Freiburg, Herder, 1952).

it is" with its ideological and idealized representation:
realism upholds the truth against concealment and
falsification. In this sense realism shows the ideal c
human freedom in its actual negation and betraya
and thus preserves the transcendence without whic
art itself is cancelled. In contrast, Soviet realism con
forms to the pattern of a repressive state. The con
scious and controlled implementation of state policie
through the medium of literature, music, painting
and so forth, is by itself not incompatible with ar
(examples could be cited from Greek art to Ber
Brecht). However, Soviet realism goes beyond th
artistic implementation of political norms by accepting
the established social reality as the final framewor.
for the artistic content, transcending it neither in
style nor in substance. Certain shortcomings, blun
ders, and lags in this reality are criticized, but neithe
the individual nor his society is referred to a spher
of fulfillment other than that prescribed by and
enclosed in the prevailing system. To be sure, the
are referred to the communist *future*, but the latte
is presented as evolving from the present withou
"exploding" the existing contradictions. The futur
is said to be nonantagonistic to the present; re
pression will gradually and through obedient effor
engender freedom and happiness—no catastroph
separates history from prehistory, the negation from
its negation. But it is precisely the catastrophic ele
ment inherent in the conflict between man's essenc
and his existence that has been the center towar
which art has gravitated since its secession from ritual
The artistic images have preserved the determinat
negation of the established reality—ultimate freedom
When Soviet aesthetics attack the notion of the "un
surmountable antagonism between essence and exist

ence" as the theoretical principle of "formalism," [7]
it thereby attacks the principle of art itself. In Marxian
theory, this antagonism is a *historical* fact, and is to
be resolved in a society which reconciles the existence
of man with his essence by providing the material
conditions for the free development of all humane
faculties. If and when this has been achieved, the
traditional basis of art would have been undermined—through the realization of the content of art.
Prior to this historical event, art retains its critical
cognitive function: to represent the still transcendental
truth, to sustain the image of freedom against a denying reality. With the realization of freedom, art would
no longer be a vessel of the truth.[8] Hegel, who saw
this realization as the task of his own period, already
proclaimed that art had become a thing of the past,
had lost its substance. He attributed this obsolescence
of art to the new scientific-philosophical spirit, which
demanded a stricter formulation of the truth than
that accessible to art.[9] Marxian theory retained the
historical link between social progress and the obsolescence of art: the development of the productive
forces renders possible the material fulfillment of the
promesse du bonheur expressed in art; political action
—the revolution—is to translate this possibility into
reality.

Soviet Marxism claims that the Bolshevik Revolution has created the basis for this translation. What
then remains as the function and content of art?

[7] V. A. Razumnyi, "O sushchnosti realisticheskogo khudoz-
hestvennogo obraza" (On the Essence of a Realistic Artistic
Form), *Voprosy Filosofii* (Problems of Philosophy), 1952,
No. 6, p. 101.
[8] Hegel, "Vorlesungen über die Aesthetik," in *Sämtliche
Werke,* ed. by H. Glockner (26 vols.; Stuttgart, F. Fromman,
1927-40), XII, 215.
[9] *Ibid.,* pp. 30, 32.

Soviet aesthetics answers: Reflection of the reality
in the form of artistic images.[1] "The law of our
aesthetics is that the more realistic our literature is
the more romantic it becomes."[2] In other words, once
the reality itself embodies the ideal (though not yet
in its pure form), art must necessarily reflect the
reality, that is, if it is to retain its essential function,
it must be "realism." The *promesse du bonheur* which,
being beyond reality, constituted the "romantic" element in art, now appears as the realistic concern of
the policy makers—realism and romanticism converge. But this convergence, if it were genuine, would
make art superfluous. The reality of freedom would
repel the ideology of freedom in its artistic transcendence. Hegel saw in the obsolescence of art a
token of progress. As the development of Reason
conquers transcendence ("takes it back" into reality)
art turns into its own negation. Soviet aesthetics
rejects this idea and insists on art, while outlawing
the transcendence of art. It wants art that is not art,
and it gets what it asks for.

However, the Soviet treatment of art is not simply
an outburst of boundless authoritarianism; its historical significance goes beyond that of political and
national requirements for regimentation. The most
shocking notions of Soviet aesthetics testify to a keen
awareness of the social function of art. They are
chiefly derived from the strong emphasis placed on
the cognitive function of art. According to Soviet
aesthetics, there is no essential contradiction and
opposition between art and science; the artistic and

[1] Razumnyi, "O sushchnosti realisticheskogo khudozhestven-
nogo obraza" (On the Essence of a Realistic Artistic Form),
Voprosy Filosofii (Problems of Philosophy), 1952, No. 6, p. 99.
[2] *Literaturnaia Gazeta* (Literary Gazette), November 17,
1948.

logical notions are inseparable.[3] In "much the
ne way as science," art expresses the "objective
th."[4] Still, art is a specific presentation of truth—
presentation which is incommensurate with scien-
c as well as common-language communication. The
sons for this incommensurability are manifold;
y seem to pertain to the fact that art reveals and
the same time consecrates the (subjectively and
ectively) unmastered forces in man and his world,
"danger zones" beneath and beyond social con-
. Viewed from the position of a repressive society,
imate freedom resides in these danger zones. On
deepest level, art is a protest against that which
By that very token, art is a "political" matter:
eft to itself, it may endanger law and order. Plato's
atment of art and his system of rigid censorship
ich fuses aesthetic, political, and epistemological
eria, does more justice to the nature and function
art than does its evaluation as "free" intellectual,
otional, or educational entertainment.

But art as a political force is art only in so far as it
serves the images of liberation; in a society which
n its totality the negation of these images, art can
serve them only by total refusal, that is, by not
cumbing to the standards of the unfree reality,
er in style, or in form, or in substance. The more
alitarian these standards become, the more reality
trols all language and all communication, the more
alistic and surrealistic will art tend to be, the more
it be driven from the concrete to the abstract,

Razumnyi, "O sushchnosti realisticheskogo khudozhestven-
obraza" (On the Essence of a Realistic Artistic Form),
rosy Filosofii (Problems of Philosophy), 1952, No. 6,
99 and 107.
P. Trofimov and others, "Printsipy marksistsko-leninskoi
tiki" (Principles of Marxist-Leninist Aesthetics), *Kom-
ist* (Communist), 1954, No. 16 (November), p. 95.

from harmony to dissonance, from content to form. /
is thus the refusal of everything that has been ma
part and parcel of reality. The works of the gr
"bourgeois" antirealists and "formalists" are far dee
committed to the idea of freedom than is socia
and Soviet realism. The irreality of their art expres
the irreality of freedom: art is as transcendental
its object. The Soviet state by administrative dec
prohibits the transcendence of art; it thus elimina
even the ideological reflex of freedom in an unf
society. Soviet realistic art, complying with the decr
becomes an instrument of social control in the l
still nonconformist dimension of the human existen
Cut off from its historical base, socialized withou
socialist reality, art reverts to its ancient prehistori
function: it assumes magical character. Thus, it
comes a decisive element in the pragmatic rational
of behaviorism.

"Art teaches . . . a definite relation toward re
ity." [5] The relation is exemplified by the "typic
images of the Soviet hero and patriot, in his strug
against hostile and obsolete forces. Soviet art aims
creating and establishing such a relation in real
and is to effectuate this relation *as art,* that is, throu
the artistic image, through the artistic illusion. I
this is the principle of magic: To "enact in fant
the fulfillment of the desired reality," "an illus
technique supplementary to the real technique." [6]
illusion, of course, cannot have a direct effect
reality, but in so far as it changes the "subject
attitude to reality," indirectly it changes reality.
regression of the cognitive function of art from

[5] *Ibid.,* pp. 107-8.
[6] George Thomson, *Studies in Ancient Greek Society* (N
York, International Publishers, 1949), p. 440. See ab
pp. 72 f.

artistic to the magical comes out in the most reactionary feature of Soviet aesthetics: the rejection of formalism" and of all "abstract" and "dissonant" structures. The progressive elements in modern "bourgeois art" were precisely in those structures which preserved the "shock" character of art,[7] that is, those expressing the catastrophic conflict. They represented the desperate attempt to break through the social standardization and falsification which had made the traditional artistic structures unusable for expressing the artistic content. The harmonious forms, in their realistic as well as classical and romantic development, had lost their transcendental, critical force; they stood no longer antagonistic to reality, but appeared as part and adornment of it—as instruments of adjustment. Communicated through the mass media, they became welcome tunes accompanying daily work and leisure, nourishment for recreation and relaxation periods. Under these circumstances, only their determinate negation could restore their content. Conversely, through the reinstatement of harmony by administrative decree, the banning of dissonance, discord, and atonality, the cognitive function of art is "brought in line," and conformity is enforced in the per se nonconformistic artistic imagination.

It is interesting to note that, with its denunciation of dissonant art, Soviet aesthetics reverts to Plato's dictum, which permits only beautiful, simple, and harmonious forms. Only these forms "mix" with the Good and the Truth: "And now the power of the good has returned into the region of the beautiful; for measure and symmetry are beauty and virtue all the world over" and "we said that truth was to form

---

[7] T. W. Adorno, "Die gegängelte Musik," in *Dissonanzen* Göttingen, Vandenhoeck und Ruprecht, 1956), pp. 46 ff.

an element in this mixture." [8] Plato's theory of ar
refers to a state in which the philosopher kings guard
the standards for the good, the true, and the beautifu
—a state antagonistic to reality. Pressed into the servic
of reality, the mixture destroys its own components

Within the general framework of the political con
trols over art, a wide range of policy modifications i
possible. Relaxation and tightening, alteration of ar
tistic standards and styles, depend on the internal and
international constellations. Naturally, with the transi
tion from terroristic to normal modes of societal regi
mentation, the claim for more artistic freedom will b
heard and perhaps fulfilled. The rigidity of "Sovie
realism" may well be loosened; realism and roman
ticism, in any case, have ceased to be opposites, and
even "formalistic" and "abstract" elements may stil
become reconcilable with conformist enjoyment. In it
societal function, art shares the growing impotence o
individual autonomy and cognition.

[8] *Philebus* 64.

7

DIALECTIC AND
ITS VICISSITUDES

Perhaps nothing is more revealing in the development of Soviet Marxism than its treatment of dialectic. Dialectical logic is the cornerstone of Marxian theory; it guides the analysis of the prerevolutionary as well as of the revolutionary development, and this analysis in turn is supposed to guide the strategy in both periods. Any fundamental "revision" of dialectical logic that goes beyond the Marxist application of dialectic to a new historical situation would indicate not only a "deviation" from Marxian theory (which is only of dogmatic interest) but also a theoretical justification for a change in the basic trend. Interpreters of Soviet theory have therefore correctly drawn attention to events in this sphere. They have concluded that Soviet Marxism has tuned down and arrested the dialectic in the interest of the ideological justification and protection of a regime which, according to dialectical logic, must appear as subject to being surpassed by the historical development. Chief support of this conclusion is seen in the emasculation of the transition from quantity to quality, the denial of explosive changes under socialism (the notion of "nonantagonistic contradictions"), in the reintroduction of formal logic, and in the disappearance from the dialectical vocabulary of the "negation of the negation." [1] In point of fact, however, Soviet Marxism is nowhere more "orthodox" than in its painful elaboration of the dialectical method; we shall see that not one of the above mentioned innovations in itself runs counter to the Marxian (and even Hegelian) dialectical logic.

But while not a single of the basic dialectical concepts has been revised or rejected in Soviet Marxism, the function of dialectic itself has undergone a significant change: it has been transformed from a mode of critical thought into a universal "world outlook" and universal method with rigidly fixed rules and regulations, and this transformation destroys the dialectic more thoroughly than any revision. The change corresponds to that of Marxism itself from theory to ideology; dialectic is vested with the magical qualities of official thought and communication. As Marxian theory ceases to be the organon of revolutionary consciousness and practice and enters the superstructure of an established system of domination, the movement of dialectical thought is codified into a philosophical system. The more problematic the relation between dialectical and formal logic becomes, the more dialectic itself becomes formal logic. The difficulties of Soviet Marxism in producing an adequate "textbook" on dialectic and logic are not only of a political nature, but the very essence of dialectics rebels against such codification. This holds true for idealistic as well as materialistic dialectics, for neither Hegel nor Marx developed dialectic as a general methodological scheme. The first step in this direction

[1] See A. Philipov, *Logic and Dialectic in the Soviet Union* (New York, Research Program on the USSR, 1952), pp. 37 f.

was made by Engels in his Dialectics of Nature (which he did not publish), and his notes have provided the skeleton for the Soviet Marxist codification.

Marx elaborated his dialectic as a conceptual tool for comprehending an inherently antagonistic society. The dissolution of the fixed and stable notions of philosophy, political economy, and sociology into their contradictory components was to "reflect" the actual structure and movement of history; dialectic was to reproduce in theory the essence of reality. And in order to reproduce it adequately, in order to provide an adequate theory of history, the traditional categories had to be redefined because they concealed rather than revealed what happened. However, the dialectical relation between the structure of thought and that of reality is more than reflection and correspondence. If Hegel consistently transgressed the clearly established distinction between thought and its object, if he talked of "contradictions" (a "logical" term) in reality, of the "movement" of concepts, of quantity "turning" into quality, he indeed stipulated not only correspondence but a specific "identity" between thought and its object—he assimilated the one with the other. But it may be assumed that the wisdom of his critics, who note that Hegel confused two essentially different realms, was not beyond the reaches of his intelligence and awareness. According to Hegel, the traditional distinction between thought and its object is "abstract" and falsifies the real relation. Thought and its object have a common denominator, which, itself "real," constitutes the substance of thought as well as of its object. This common denominator is the inherent structure and the *telos* of all being, i.e., Reason. It is for Hegel the structure according to which all modes of being, subjective as well as ob-

jective, are modes of self-realization in an ever more
conscious form—from the "blind" process of unor-
ganic nature to the free realization of man in history.
Reason is subjective as well as objective—the Logos
of all being. It is dialectical in so far as the realization
takes place through the development and solution of
contradictions which define the various modes and
conditions of being. Being is in its essence a process
of "comprehending"—the process in which an object
becomes what it is through constituting itself (as this
particular object) in and against the various conditions and relations of its existence. By virtue of this
process, existence becomes comprehending, the object
becomes "subject," and comprehending, the "notion"
(*Begriff*), becomes the essential "reality" of being.
Self-conscious thinking is only the highest mode of an
existence common to all being, and the movement of
thought is only the highest and most general mode of
the movement of all being. Hegel speaks of one notion
turning into another, meaning that a notion, thought
through, reveals contents which at first seem alien
and even opposed to this notion. What happens is not
that in the thought process one notion is replaced by
another, by one more adequate to reality, but that
the same notion unfolds its own content—a dynamic
which *is* that of the reality comprehended in the
notion. The reality has (or rather is) its own Logos
and logic is ontology. Behind this apparent play with
the equivocation of words lies the very idea which
has been constitutive of Western philosophy since the
Greeks—the idea of the *Logos* as the essence of being,
which in turn determines the logical structure of
"definition" and makes "logic" into an instrument for
finding and communicating the truth. No matter how
inadequate the translation of Logos as "reason" may

be, it elucidates the decisive implication of this idea, namely, that the order of the cosmos (nature as well as society, physics as well as history) is at one and the same time a logical and ontological, a comprehending and comprehended (*begreifende* and *begrifene*) order. Thus the cognitive relation is constitutive of reality, is subjective *and* objective. However, the unity of the subjective and objective world is not a fact, not a given condition, but one that is to be attained in the struggle against adverse, denying conditions. Once this struggle becomes the self-conscious node of existence, namely, in the human being, the dialectical process becomes the historical process— theory and practice in one. It comes to fruition in a "state of the world" where the conflict is resolved in the transparent harmony of subject and object, individual and universal. This is the inner logic of philosophy as well as reality. The dialectical logic may thus be called a logic of *freedom*, or rather, to be more exact, a logic of *liberation*, for the process is that of an alienated world, whose "substance" can become "subject" (as the *Phenomenology of the Spirit* formulates the thesis of Hegel's philosophy) only through shattering and surpassing the conditions which "contradict" its realization. Then, however, Hegel's dialectic surpasses the historical process itself and makes it into a part of a metaphysical system in which ultimate freedom is only the freedom of the Idea.

The Marxian "inversion" of Hegel's dialectic remains committed to history. The driving forces behind the historical process are not mere conflicts but contradictions because they constitute the very Logos of history as the history of alienation. Thus, according to Marx (the Logos of) capitalist society speaks against itself: Its economy functions normally only

through periodic crises; growing productivity of labo
sustains scarcity and toil; increasing wealth perpetuate
poverty; progress is dehumanization. Specifically, a
Marx claims to show in *Capital*, it is the free wag
contract and the just exchange of equivalents whic'
generate exploitation and inequality; it is the capitalis
realization of freedom, equality, and justice whic'
turns them into their opposite.[2] The rationality o
the system is self-contradictory: the very laws whic'
govern it lead to its destruction. As in Hegel's concep
tion, the process of liberation appears not as an ex
traneous scheme superimposed upon reality but as it
objective dynamic, and the latter is the realization o
the free "subject," which now finds its historical forr
and task—that of the proletariat. Moreover, the Marx
ian dialectic also is, as a political-historical process,
cognitive one: the true consciousness (class conscious
ness) of the proletariat is a constitutive factor in th
objective dynamic of liberation.

These brief comments on the structure of dialecti
may illustrate the fate it underwent in Soviet Marxisrr
The Logos of dialectic is no longer that of liberation–
neither in Hegel's ontological nor in Marx's historica
sense. This is inevitable once dialectic is no longe
focused on the contradictions of class society but ex
tended beyond them. As Marxian theory is trans
formed into a general scientific "world outlook," dialec
tic becomes an abstract "theory of knowledge." Al
though it is to pertain to the proletariat and the Com
munist Party,[3] the connection is no longer transparent
Now Marxian theory may perhaps be called a "worl
outlook," but then its world is that of "pre-history,

---

[2] *Capital*, I, Chap. 4, conclusion.
[3] See the report on the results of the discussion of logic i
Voprosy Filosofii (Problems of Philosophy), 1951, No. (
pp. 143-49.

class society, and, specifically, capitalist society. Marxian theory analyzes and criticizes this world in all its manifestations, in its material and intellectual culture. There is no Marxian theory which may be meaningfully called a "world outlook" for postcapitalist societies—whether they be socialist or not. There is no Marxian theory of socialism because the antagonistic-dialectical laws which govern presocialist history are not applicable to the history of free mankind, and theory cannot predetermine the laws of freedom. Nor does Marxian theory "prophesy" beyond demonstrable trends in capitalist society. The essentially historical character of Marxian theory precludes unhistorical generalizations. Although Engels defined dialectic as the "science of the general laws of motion and development of nature, human society, and thought," [4] he noted that nature as well as society are "phases of historical development," and that the laws of dialectic are "abstracted" from their history.[5] In such abstraction, they can be presented as a series of general assumptions, categories, and conclusions—but the general scheme immediately cancels itself, for its categories come to life only in their historical concretion.

Consequently, in trying to present dialectic "as such," Soviet Marxists can do nothing but distill from the concrete dialectical analysis of the "classics" certain principles, illustrate them, and confront them with "undialectical" thought. The principles are those enumerated in Stalin's "Dialectical and Historical Materialism," which, in turn, are only a paraphrase of Engels's propositions in his *Dialectics of Nature*.[6] In

[4] "Anti-Dühring," in *A Handbook of Marxism*, ed. by E. Burns (New York, International Publishers, 1935), p. 266.
[5] *Dialectics of Nature*, trans. by Clemens Dutt (New York, International Publishers, 1940), p. 26.
[6] *Ibid*. For the "omission" of the "negation of the negation" see below, pp. 137 f.

terms of Hegel's and Marx's dialectic, they are neither
true nor false—they are empty shells. Hegel could
develop the principles of dialectic in the medium of
universality, as a "science of logic," because to him
the structure and movement of being was that of the
"notion" and attained its truth in the Absolute Idea;
Marxian theory, however, which rejects Hegel's interpretation of being in terms of the Idea, can no longer
unfold the dialectic as logic: its Logos is the historical
reality, and its universality is that of history.

The problem as to whether or not the Marxian
dialectic is applicable to nature must here at least be
mentioned because the emphasis on the dialectic of
nature is a distinguishing feature of Soviet Marxism—
in contrast to Marx and even to Lenin. If the Marxian
dialectic is in its conceptual structure a dialectic of
the historical reality, then it includes nature in so far
as the latter is itself part of the historical reality (in
the interaction [*Stoffwechsel*] between man and nature, the domination and exploitation of nature, nature
as ideology, etc.). But precisely in so far as nature is
investigated in abstraction from these historical relations, as in the natural sciences, it seems to lie outside
the realm of dialectic. It is no accident that in Engels's
Dialectics of Nature the dialectical concepts appear
as mere analogies, figurative and superimposed upon
the content—strikingly empty or commonplace compared with the exact concreteness of the dialectical
concepts in the economic and socio-historical writings.
And it is the *Dialectics of Nature* which has become
the constantly quoted authoritative source for the
exposition of dialectic in Soviet Marxism. Inevitably
so, for if "dialectic reigns everywhere," [7] if it is the

[7] K. S. Bakradze, "K voprosu o sootnoshenii logiki i dialektiki"
(On the Relationship Between Logic and Dialectic), *Voprosy
Filosofii* (Problems of Philosophy), 1950, No. 2, p. 200.

science of the "general laws of the material world and of knowledge," [8] and therefore the only true "scientific world outlook," then the dialectical concepts must first and foremost be validated in the most scientific of all sciences—that of nature. The consequence is a de-emphasis of history.

The Soviet Marxist hypostatization of dialectic into a universal scientific world outlook entails the division of Marxian theory into dialectical and historical materialism, the latter being the "extension" and "application" of the former to the "study of society and its history." [9] The division would have been meaningless to Marx, for whom dialectical materialism was synonymous with historical materialism. In Soviet Marxism, historical materialism becomes one particular branch of the general scientific and philosophical system of Marxism which, codified into an ideology and interpreted by the officials of the Party, justifies policy and practice. History, which in Marxian theory is the determining and validating dimension of dialectic, is in Soviet Marxism a special field in which historical as well as suprahistorical laws assert themselves. The latter, arranged into a system of propositions, are presented as the ultimately determining forces in history as well as nature. The dialectical process thus interpreted is no longer in a strict sense a historical process—it is rather that history is reified into a second nature. Soviet developments thereby obtain the dignity of the objective natural laws by which they are allegedly governed and which, if correctly understood and

[8] V. S. Molodtsov, "Ob oshibkakh v ponimanii predmeta dialekticheskogo materializma" (On False Conceptions of the Subject of Dialectical Materialism), *Voprosy Filosofii* (Problems of Philosophy), 1956, No. 1, p. 188.

[9] Stalin, "Dialectical and Historical Materialism," in *History of the Communist Party of the Soviet Union* (New York, International Publishers, 1939), p. 105.

taken into consciousness, will eventually right all
wrongs and lead to final victory over the opposing
forces.

But while the objective, determinist character of
dialectical laws is thus strengthened, Soviet Marxism
in reality appears as defying determinism and practicing voluntarism. The shift in emphasis from the
former to the latter seems to be a feature of Leninism
and seems to culminate in Stalinism. A straight road
seems to lead from Lenin's "consciousness from without" and his notion of the centralized authoritarian
party to Stalin's personal dictatorship—a road on
which "scientific determinism" gives way (in practice,
if not in ideology) to decisions on the ground of
shifting political and even personal objectives and interests. Subjective factors prevail over the objective
factors and laws. However, closer analysis shows that
the abstract opposition of determinism and voluntarism
is untenable; their interrelation is more complex and
requires discussion to the extent that it sheds light on
the socio-historical changes reflected in Soviet Marxism.

The two elements are present from the beginning in
the Marxian doctrine; their relative weight depends on
the historical conditions under which Marxism operates.[1] In periods of acute class struggles, when the
revolution is "on the agenda" and when a mature,
class-conscious proletariat is in political action, Marxism appears as little more than the conscious manifestation of objective factors. In so far as the latter tend
"by themselves" toward revolution, in so far as the
capitalist structure is shaken by economic crises and
political upheavals, Marxism can interpret the situation chiefly in terms of the harmony of the subjective
and objective factors. The function of the Marxist

[1] For the following see above, pp. 3 f.

parties and of their leadership and international organization then is to comprehend and explain the objective constellation of political forces and to direct the action of the proletariat in accordance with it. This function is a subjective factor: itself cognition and volition, it appeals to cognition and volition. However, as a subjective factor, it is only the formulation of the objective factors, which, directing the political action, becomes an integral part and aspect of them. In contrast, when the revolutionary potential is weakened, absorbed, or defeated, then the cognitive and voluntarist element is not embodied in the objective situation. The consciousness and action of the proletariat then are largely determined by the "blind laws" of the capitalist process instead of having broken through this determinism. Consequently, the party, or rather the party leadership, appears as the historical repository of the "true" interests of the proletariat and above the proletariat, working by dictum and decree, and the proletariat becomes the object of these decisions. The subjective and objective factors are torn asunder—in reality, and this development appears in theory as the tension and antagonism between voluntarism and determinism.

It has often been noted that Marxian theory underwent a significant change after 1848. The philosophic humanism of the earlier writings, in which socialism is defined in terms of human aspirations and potentialities, gave way to a "scientific socialism governed by inexorable objective laws." [2] The transformation reflects the actual situation of the proletariat. The determinist elements in Marxian theory pertain to the structure of class society and particularly to capitalism,

[2] See Leonard Krieger, "Marx and Engels as Historians," *Journal of the History of Ideas*, XIV, No. 3 (June, 1953), 396 ff.

where men are subordinated to unmastered forces, operating "behind the back of the individuals" as inexorable laws. The abortive revolutions of 1848 and the ensuing consolidation of bourgeois society reasserted the "validity" of these laws, to which the bulk of the proletariat also succumbed. While Marxian theory reflects this extended determinism by increasing emphasis on the scientific character of the dialectic toward socialism, the "voluntarist" element comes to reside in a separate historical agency or agent, that is, in the leadership. The "true" consciousness is that which has not succumbed to the "false" determinism. But no matter how great the distance may be between the consciousness of the leadership and that of the proletariat, the former, in its theory and practice, must retain or reestablish the demonstrable connection between the "immediate" and the "real" interest of the proletariat. This relation between a highly centralized leadership and the proletariat which remains its determining base is illustrated in the period of the First International. At that time, the ideas, objectives, and attitudes of the leadership were remote from those of the proletariat and certainly not shared or even understood by the great majority of the latter. Still, the Inaugural Address, the analyses of the Paris Commune, and the communications of the leadership testify to the extent to which the factual attitude and actions of the proletariat determined the leadership's theory and strategy.

Subsequently, as ever larger strata of the industrial proletariat were installed in the capitalist system and partook of its benefits, the "natural laws" governing the system also seemed to engulf its negation. Revisionist Marxism affirmed this process. Dialectic was discarded. Eduard Bernstein's doctrine implied a determinism far more rigid than that of Marx and Engels. The subjective factor was objectified at the expense of its revolutionary content and intent: the proletariat moved—with the whole of society—under objective laws toward socialism, and the leadership operated under the same laws. We have tried to show above how Leninism attempted to restore the true relation between the subjective and objective factors by establishing the authority of the centralized revolutionary party over and above the proletariat. Again, the strengthening of the voluntarist element was accompanied by a strengthening of the determinist character of Marxian theory: Lenin's *Materialism and Empirio-criticism* replaced the dialectical notion of truth by a primitive naturalistic realism, which has become canonical in Soviet Marxism. However, in Leninism, the two factors remained closely related: during the Revolution, it became apparent to what degree Lenin had succeeded in basing his strategy on the actual class interests and aspirations of the workers and peasants. At the same time, the dialectic was reactivated and provided the conceptual tools for Lenin's guiding analyses of the historical situation. Then, from 1923 on, the decisions of the leadership have been increasingly dissociated from the class interests of the proletariat. The former no longer presuppose the proletariat as a revolutionary agent but rather are imposed upon the proletariat and the rest of the underlying population. The authoritarian voluntarism which characterized the Stalinist leadership responds to the objective determinant, the reduction of the revolutionary potential in the capitalist countries. And as the will of the leadership acts upon the proletariat from above, the theory pronounced by the leadership or endorsed by it assumes rigid determinist

forms. The dialectic is petrified into a universal system
in which the historical process appears as a "natural"
process and in which objective laws over and above
the individuals govern not only the capitalist but also
the socialist society. The fate of the dialectic reveals
the historical substance of Soviet society: it is not
the negation of capitalism, but it partakes, in a decisive aspect, of the function of capitalism, namely,
in the industrial development of the productive forces
under separation of the control of production from
the "immediate producers." Soviet theory here expresses what the ideology denies: that the Bolshevik
Revolution did "not yet" entail a socialist revolution,
that the "first phase" is not yet socialism. But while
Soviet society thus partakes of the function of capitalism, it does so on an economic foundation—total
nationalization—which makes for an essentially different developmental tendency beyond the present
framework, in a direction which we shall subsequently
try to identify. Now, we shall briefly illustrate the
petrification of the dialectic and the points at which
the future trend seems to become manifest.

The exposition of the dialectic in the representative
textbooks is focused on the determinist character of
the dialectical process. For example, in Rozental's
Marksistskii Dialekticheskii Metod (Marxist Dialectical Method), the capitalist development, the transition to socialism, and the subsequent development of
Soviet society through its various phases is presented
as the unfolding of a system of objective forces that
could not have unfolded otherwise. To be sure,
strong and constant emphasis is placed on the guiding
role of the Communist Party and its leaders, and on
the patriotic heroism of the Soviet people, but their
action and its success was made possible only by

their understanding of an obedience to the inexorable laws of dialectic. The subjective factor no longer appears as an integral element and stage of the objective dialectic, but rather as the mere vessel, recipient, or executor of the latter. This notion has remained obligatory during and after the Stalinist era. The Party and the Party leadership are the sole authority for the interpretation of dialectic—but this independence is qualified: the leaders themselves are subject to the objective laws which they interpret and implement.

The particular role of ideology in socialist society is determined by the nature of the development of this society, which differs essentially from the nature of the development of previous [social] formations. Under socialism, too, the laws of the social development are objective ones, *operating independently from the consciousness and will of human beings,* but under socialism, the party, the state, and society as a whole have the opportunity, unknown in past history, of comprehending these laws, consciously applying them in their activities, and, by this very token, accelerating the course of societal development.[3]

The Soviet Marxist interpretation of the relation between the subjective and objective factor transforms the dialectical process into a mechanistic one. This becomes particularly clear in the discussion of the relation between necessity and freedom. It is the key problem in the Hegelian as well as the Marxian dialectic, and we have seen that it is also a key problem in the idea of socialism itself. Soviet Marx-

[3] M. T. Iovchuk, "Rol' sotsialisticheskoi ideologii v bor'be s perezhitkami kapitalizma" (The Role of Socialist Ideology in the Struggle with Survivals of Capitalism), *Voprosy Filosofii* (Problems of Philosophy), 1955, No. 1, p. 4 (italics added). Emphasis on the subordination of the Soviet state to the objective laws of the historical process is one of the essential points in Stalin's last article; see above, pp. 106 f.

ism defines freedom as "recognized necessity." [4] The formula follows Engels's restatement of Hegel's definition according to which freedom is "insight into necessity." [5] But for Hegel, freedom is not merely "insight" into necessity, but is comprehended (*begriffene*) necessity, which implies a change in the actual conditions. Mere "insight" can never change necessity into freedom; Hegel's "comprehended" necessity is "not merely the freedom of abstract negation, but rather concrete and positive freedom"—only thus is it the "truth" of necessity. The transition from necessity to freedom is that into a fundamentally different dimension of "being," and Hegel calls it the "hardest" of all dialectical transitions.[6]

Soviet Marxism minimizes this transition and assimilates freedom to necessity—in ideology as well as in reality. This assimilation is expressed in the Soviet Marxist interpretation of dialectical change, that is, of the development from one stage of class society to another. In Marxian theory, this development is (*a*) *catastrophic* (the unfolding contradictions of class society can be resolved only by explosion), and (*b*) as catastrophic development it is *progressive* (the stage initiated by the revolution is a higher stage of civilization). However, both these elements are themselves subjective as well as objective factors. The "explosion" is not automatic but presupposes the action and the consciousness of the revolutionary

[4] For example, M. D. Kammari, "O novom vydaiushchemsia vklade I. V. Stalina v marksistsko-leninskuiu filosofiiu" (On the Distinguished New Contribution by J. V. Stalin to Marxist-Leninist Philosophy), *Voprosy Filosofii* (Problems of Philosophy), 1952, No. 6, p. 32.
[5] "Anti-Dühring," in *Handbook of Marxism*, pp. 255 f.
[6] *Encyclopädie der philosophischen Wissenschaften im Grundrisse*, I, par. 158 and 159; *Science of Logic*, Book II, Sect. 3, Chap. 3, C.

class; and "progress" denotes only the development of the productive forces and continues to involve exploitation and enslavement until the proletariat has become the historical agent.[7]

Into this conception, Soviet Marxism introduces the distinction between antagonistic and nonantagonistic contradictions ("conflicts" and "contradictions"):[8] the former irreconcilable and "soluble" only through a catastrophic explosion; the latter subject to gradual solution through political control; the former characteristic of class society, the latter characteristic of socialist society. Soviet Marxism claims that the change from the explosive to the gradual dialectical transition has been rendered possible in the USSR with the establishment of the Soviet state. In line with this conception, and following Stalin's example of 1938, the "law of the negation of the negation" disappeared from the list of the fundamental dialectical laws. Quite obviously, the Soviet Marxist conception of dialectic is most suitable to serve the ideological stabilization of the established state: it assigns to the state the historical task of solving the "nonantagonistic

[7] See for example, Marx to Ruge, September, 1843, in "Deutsch-Französische Jahrbücher I," in Marx and Engels, *Historisch-Kritische Gesamtausgabe,* ed. by D. Rjazonov (Frankfurt, Marx-Engels Archiv Verlagsgesellschaft, 1927), Div. I. I, Pt. 1, 575; and Marx and Engels, *The German Ideology* (New York, International Publishers, 1939), p. 7.

[8] See for example M. M. Rozental, *Marksistskii dialekticheskii metod* (Marxist Dialectical Method) (Moscow, Gospolitizdat, 1951), *passim;* S. P. Dudel, "K voprosy o edinstve i bor'be protivepolonovsti: kak vnutrennem soderzhanii protsessa razvitia" (On the Question of the Unity and Struggle of Opposites as the Content of the Process of Development), in *Voprosy Dialekticheskogo Materializma* (Questions of Dialectical Materialism) (Moscow, Akademia Nauk SSSR, 1951) pp. 73 ff. The Soviet Marxist doctrine of dialectical contradictions took final shape after Zhdanov's speech against G. F. Aleksandrov, June 1947, printed in *Bol'shevik* (Bolshevik), 1947, No. 16 (August 30) pp. 7-23.

contradictions" and precludes theoretically the necessity of another revolution on the way to communism.
It should be noted, however, that the Soviet Marxist
revision is theoretically consistent with the Marxian
conception. According to Marx, the "catastrophic"
character of the transition from quantity to quality
belongs to the realm of blindly operating, uncontrolled
socio-economic forces; with the establishment of socialism, these forces come under the rational control
of society as a whole, which self-consciously regulates
its struggle with nature and with its own contradictions. Moreover, the change in the mode of transition
from one stage to another is already stipulated in
Hegel's system: once the level of free and self-
conscious rationality has been reached ("being-in-
and-for-itself"), such rationality also governs the
further transitions at this level. Similarly, Marx applied the notion of the "negation of the negation"
specifically to the capitalist development. It is the
"capitalist production" which, with the necessity of
a "law of nature" engenders its own negation: socialism is this "negation of the negation." [9] The dialectical
method does not stipulate the schematic repetition of
this concept, and Hegel warns explicitly against
the formalistic interpretation and application of the
"triad." [1] The Soviet Marxist "revision" is "orthodox."
Since Soviet Marxists maintain that Soviet society is
a socialist society, they consistently invest it with
the corresponding dialectical characteristics. What
is involved is not so much a revision of dialectic as
the claim of socialism for a nonsocialist society.
Dialectic itself is used for substantiating this claim.

All this seems to confirm that the Soviet Marxist

[9] *Capital*, I, Chap. 24.
[1] *Science of Logic*, Book III, Sect. 3, Chap. 3.

treatment of dialectic merely serves to protect and justify the established regime by eliminating or minimizing all those elements of dialectic which would indicate progress of the socio-historical development beyond this regime, that is, toward a qualitatively different higher stage of socialism. In other words, Soviet Marxism would represent the "arresting" of dialectic in the interest of the prevailing state of affairs—the ideology would follow the arresting of socialism in reality.

However, the situation is more complicated. We have noted at the beginning that Soviet ideology and reality are subject to a dynamic which the regime cannot arrest without undermining its own foundations. We have suggested that the international development tends to force the Soviet regime to direct its efforts toward the "second phase" of socialism—a trend which would also tend to alter the "superstructure." In line with the assimilation of ideology to reality, the trend would not only be noticeable but perhaps even anticipated in ideology. Recent developments in the Soviet Marxist treatment of dialectic seem to corroborate this assumption. Even during the last period of Stalinism, it appeared that ideological preparations were being made for rendering the regime more flexible, for "normalizing" it and for orienting Soviet society toward a long period of economic as well as political "coexistence"—a period required for the further internal growth of the Soviet system. The Soviet Marxist discussion of dialectic seems designed to adjust the ideology to the new period.

We have mentioned Stalin's reiterated emphasis on the "active" role of the superstructure in developing its base; this is not merely the ideological justi-

fication and stabilization of a prevailing form and
stage of the state but also the ideological commitment
of the state to introduce changes in conformity with
the growth of the productive forces. As such, Stalin's
statement of 1950 pointed toward his "Economic
Problems of Socialism" [2] of 1952, with the stress on
the contradictions between productive forces and
production relations in the USSR, to be solved "gradually" under the guidance of the state. Similarly, the
discussion of logic and dialectic in 1950-1951 seems
not so much an ideological defense of the status quo
against potential change, a protection from historical
progress, as a preparation for intended changes. The
discussion of the relation between formal and dialectical logic was linked throughout with Stalin's
pronouncements in "Marxism and Linguistic Problems." [3] There Stalin had pointed out that it is
"un-Marxist" and incorrect to talk of the "class conditioning" of language and to envisage a specifically
"socialist language." He had maintained that language
"differs in principle from a superstructure" in that
it does not change with the base but outlives this
or that base; it is created by and "serves," not certain
classes, but society as a whole over the course of
centuries. By the same token, Soviet Marxism declared, it is incorrect to treat formal logic as "class
conditioned" and to envisage a specific "Soviet logic"
corresponding to the new basis of Soviet society. [4]
The report on the results of the discussion on logic
sums up:

[2] In *Current Soviet Policies,* ed. by Leo Gruliow (New
York, F. A. Praeger, 1953), pp. 1-20.
[3] See Stalin, *Marksizm i voprosy iazykoznaniia* (Marxism
and Linguistic Problems) (Moscow, Gospolitizdat, 1950).
[4] V. I. Cherkesov, "O logike i marksistskoi dialektike" (On
Logic and Marxist Dialectic), *Voprosy Filosofii* (Problems of
Philosophy), 1950, No. 2, p. 211.

The logical forms and laws of thought are no super-structure over and above the base. . . . Formal logic is the science of the elementary laws and forms of correct thinking. . . . There are not two logics: an old meta-physical, and a new, dialectical logic. . . . There is only one formal logic, which is universally valid.[5]

Dialectical logic does not deny, cancel, or contradict the validity of formal logic; the former belongs to a different dimension of knowledge and is related to the latter as higher to elementary mathematics.

We are not concerned here with the course and conclusions of the discussion.[6] Significantly, the chang-ing trend announces itself in a return to Marxian orthodoxy after the leftist "Marrist deviations." In terms of Marxian theory, neither language nor logic as such belong to the superstructure; they belong rather to the preconditions of the basic societal relationships themselves: as instruments of communi-cation and knowledge, they are indispensable for establishing and sustaining these relationships. Only certain manifestations of language and thought are superstructure, as for example, in art, philosophy, religion. Following the Marxian conception, the Soviet discussion distinguished between logic itself and the *sciences* of logic. As a specific interpretation of logic, some of the latter must be classified as ideological.[7] Neither the Hegelian nor the Marxian dialectic denied

[5] *Voprosy Filosofii* (Problems of Philosophy), 1951, No. 6, pp. 145, 146.
[6] They are summarized, in *ibid.*, pp. 143-49, and in Gustav Wetter, *Der Dialektische Materialismus* (Freiburg, Herder, 1952), pp. 544 ff. For the post-Stalin development see George L. Kline, "Recent Soviet Philosophy," in American Academy of Political Science, *Annals*, CCCIII (January, 1956), 126-38.
[7] I. I. Osmakov, "O zakone myshleniia i o nauke logiki" (On the Law of Thinking and on the Science of Logic), *Voprosy Filosofii* (Problems of Philosophy), 1950, No. 3, pp. 318 ff.

the validity of formal logic; rather they preserved and validated its truth by unfolding its content in the dialectical conception which reveals the necessary abstractness of "common" as well as "scientific" sense.

Compared with this tradition of dialectic, "Marrist"[8] linguistic and logic (which stressed to the extreme the class character of both) must indeed appear as a gross "leftist deviation," as an "infantile disease" of communism in its age of immaturity. It seemed to be an ideological by-product of the first phase of the Stalinist construction of socialism in one country. The violent struggle to overcome the technological and industrial backwardness of the country, imposed by terror upon a largely passive and even hostile population, found its ideological compensation in the various doctrines of the uniqueness and superiority of Soviet man, deriving from his "possession" of Marxism as the only true and progressive "world outlook." But Marxian theory is in its very substance international. Within its framework, nationalism is progressive only as a stage in the historical process—a stage which, according to Marx and Engels, had already been surpassed by the advanced Western world. Soviet Marxism has never succeeded in reconciling the contradiction between its own nationalism and Marxian internationalism—either in its strategy or in its ideology, as is demonstrated by the painful distinctions between "bourgeois cosmopolitanism" and genuine internationalism, between chauvinism and "Soviet patriotism." Moreover, the emphasis on a special Soviet mentality, logic, linguistic, and so forth, was bound to impair the appeal to international solidarity in the ultimate revolutionary objective as

[8] Only the Stalinist evaluation of Marr's doctrines is here discussed, not the doctrines themselves.

well as the appeal for peaceful coexistence, which the doctrine of socialism or communism in one country could not discard altogether. The "Marrist" theories may have fulfilled a useful function in the "magical" utilization of Marxian theory, but with the technological and industrial progress of Soviet society, with the growing political and strategic power of the Soviet state, they came into conflict with more fundamental objectives. As Soviet policy began to be oriented to the transition to the "second phase," the Marrist doctrines had to give way to more universalist, "normal," and internationalist conceptions. Far from signifying the "arrest" of dialectic in the interest of the stabilization of the attained level of development, the reiteration of the common human function and content of language and logic seems to be aimed at bringing the ideology in line with the drive toward the "next higher stage" of the development, that is, the second phase of socialism, and with the policy of "normalizing" East-West relations involved in this transition.

8

THE TRANSITION FROM
SOCIALISM
TO COMMUNISM

The entire Soviet Marxist interpretation of dialectic is, as all ideological efforts since the last period of Stalinism are, focused on the transition from socialism to communism (or from the first to the second phase of communist society—the two formulations are used interchangeably). The idea of this transition has been an essential element of Soviet Marxism ever since the consolidation of the Soviet state after the first Five-Year Plan. As early as 1935, in his speech to the First All-Union Conference of Stakhanovites, Stalin hailed the Stakhanov movement as "preparing the conditions for the transition from Socialism to Communism," "the first beginnings—still feeble, it is true, but nevertheless the beginnings" of that "rise in the cultural and technical level of the working class of our country" which is the prerequisite for the "second phase." [1] But while the idea of this transition (without which Soviet Marxism could not even claim to be

[1] *Leninism* (New York, International Publishers, 1942), pp. 367 and 369.

Marxism) has accompanied the construction of socialism in one country from the beginning, the transition is now presented as being in process, as the next objective of Soviet domestic policy. This is the gist of Stalin's last publication "Economic Problems of Socialism in the USSR," which was then appraised by Soviet Marxism as the first authoritative Marxist theory of the concrete forms of this transition. The article retains its significance in spite of the critique to which it was subjected at the Twentieth Congress.

Implied is a "normal" development, that is, no war with the West. In accord with this presupposition, Stalin insisted on the precedence of interimperialist conflicts over the conflict between the capitalist and the socialist orbit. A whole section is devoted to the affirmation of the "inevitability" of wars among capitalist countries.[2] Apparently for the first time, Stalin cited publicly a Soviet Marxist analysis (referred to as that of "some comrades") of contemporary capitalism, which holds that the intercontinental integration of capitalism after the Second World War is not merely an extraneous political constellation, but is founded on a basis which makes wars among the capitalist countries no longer inevitable. This notion, which amounts to a denial of the Marxist-Leninist theory of imperialism, is cited only to be *rejected*. In his rejection, Stalin insisted on the reactivation of the economic conflicts between the United States on the one side, and the "subservient" capitalist countries on the other (Britain and France primarily;

[2] "Economic Problems of Socialism in the USSR," in *Current Soviet Policies*, ed. by Leo Gruliow (New York, F. A. Praeger, 1953), pp. 7 f. For the following discussion see above, pp. 50 ff.

but also Germany and Japan). On the other hand, war between the imperialist and the Soviet camp is *not* inevitable.

The modification of the thesis on the "inevitability of war" is highly ambiguous. First of all, in traditional Marxist usage, it refers primarily to wars among *capitalist* countries. As such, the thesis is in the center of the doctrine of imperialism. Conversely, the "correction" of the thesis refers primarily to wars between the imperialist and the Soviet camps: the war that is no longer inevitable is this East-West war. Once this ambiguity is cleared up, there appears to be a strange consistency in the Stalinist and post-Stalinist conception. The statements on the sharpening of the intracapitalist contradictions made at the Twentieth Congress[3] are substantively (and sometimes even literally) in line with the Stalinist formulas! The consistency is explained by the main point at which post-Stalinist policy continues and strengthens late Stalinist policy, namely, by the reliance on "normal" capitalist development, stabilization of East-West relations, internal growth of Soviet society, and economic-political competition. The war whose evitability is now so strongly emphasized is first of all the war between capitalist and socialist countries. It can be prevented by virtue of the increased power of the socialist camp and the latter's impact upon the "peace-loving" populations in the capitalist countries. However, these very same factors in turn would tend to counteract war in general—therefore,

[3] See the statements by Mikoyan and Khrushchev at the Twentieth Party Congress, in *XX S"ezd Kommunisticheskoi Partii Sovetskogo Soiuza; Stenograficheskii otchet* (The Twentieth Congress of the Communist Party of the Soviet Union; Stenographic Account) (2 vols.; Moscow, Gospolitizdat, 1956), I, 14-20, 319-21.

even war between capitalist countries would seem
no longer "inevitable."

The shift in the Soviet Marxist position on the
inevitability of war thus seems thoroughly consistent.
As compared with the period when Lenin asserted
the inevitability of imperialist wars, the internal and
international situations have changed fundamentally,
and a "balance of power" has been established (i.e.,
the strength of the Soviet camp), which serves as a
deterrent against an East-West war. But this same
deterring force has also reduced the possibility of
military conflicts within the imperialist camp (from
which the Soviet camp would emerge as beneficiary),
while aggravating the economic and political difficulties in the capitalist world.

We have seen that this thesis on the aggravating
capitalist contradictions belongs to the hard core of
Soviet Marxism. However, the context in which
Stalin repeated it in his last article gave it a special
significance. The proposition introduces the discussion
of the transition from socialism to communism as the
next phase in the development of Soviet society. In
this context, the proposition serves to reiterate the
priority of domestic over foreign policy. In the first
representative article on Soviet foreign policy after
Stalin's death, *Kommunist* recalled that, according
to Marxism-Leninism, "the foreign policy of any state
is a continuation of its domestic policy and is governed
by it." [4] For the USSR, this "normal" Marxist-Leninist
constellation was interrupted by the Second World
War, the subsequent strategic adjustments, and the
period of restoration. The Nineteenth Party Congress
seems to herald the return to the normal supremacy

[4] 1953, No. 7, translated in *Current Digest of the Soviet Press,*
V, No. 20 (June 27, 1953), 3.

of domestic policy and to initiate its new phase. We have stressed that the discussion of Stalin's article in *Voprosy Ekonomiki* (Problems of Economics) explicitly states that "in actuality," the interimperialist conflicts supersede the conflict between the imperialist and the Soviet camp.[5] This portion of Stalin's article has remained mandatory for the party line: the conflicts among the imperialist powers and within the imperialist countries make for a "peaceful" internal reduction of capitalist strength.

> The aggressive foreign policy of the USA sharpens the contradictions in the very camp of imperialism. . . . Soviet foreign policy . . . cannot refuse to take into account both the presence of considerable contradictions between individual capitalist countries and the presence of contradictions within these countries and even within individual parties adhering to capitalist classes and groups. It is our task to utilize these contradictions for the sake of preserving and solidifying peace and weakening the aggressive, anti-democratic forces.[6]

The imperialist policy of strength is now opposed— so the argument runs—not only by the broad masses of the people but also by a part of the "well-to-do classes." [7] While one should not underestimate the danger that a small "handful of exploiters" may unleash war out of sheer desperation, "it would be a still greater mistake to overestimate imperialism's forces." [8]

While the reevaluation of the interimperialist situation suggests a new trend in foreign policy, the

[5] See above, p. 49.

[6] "Za uprochenie mira mezhdu narodami" (For the Consolidation of Peace Between Peoples), *Kommunist* (Communist), 1955, No. 4 (March), p. 12.

[7] "Sud'by mira i tsivilizatsii reshaiut narody" (The Peoples Decide the Fates of Peace and of Civilization), *Kommunist* (Communist), 1955, No. 4 (March), p. 12.

[8] *Ibid.*, p. 18.

discussion of the economic problems of socialism indicates the internal basis (and perhaps also the reason) for this trend. The reorientation in foreign policy seems to have been necessitated by a domestic reorientation. The attainment of the international objectives—chiefly the weakening of Western society from within—ultimately depends on the attainment of a higher level of Soviet society (in Marxist language, the second stage of socialism).[9] Stalin's political testament reformulated Lenin's in terms of this transition: it stipulated the need for a new prolonged "respite" as the prerequisite for the further development of Soviet society.

In the "Economic Problems of Socialism," Stalin's proposition on the inevitability of interimperialist conflicts is followed by his definition of the "basic economic law of present-day capitalism," that is, the "need to obtain maximum profit." Stalin contrasts this "law" with the "law of the average profit norm" that was valid for the preceding stages of the capitalist development. Marxist interpreters of this passage have been troubled by the question of orthodoxy involved here: in Marxian terms, the need for maximum profit is inherent in the capitalist mode of production itself and cannot be contrasted with the "law of the average profit norm" because either it is subject to the latter law or it remains an exception—pertaining only to "privileged" groups of enterprises. Soviet commentators have disregarded this difficulty and taken Stalin's formulation as a cue for redefining the situation of present-day capitalism.

The notion of the "second phase" of the general crisis of capitalism,[1] as formulated by this redefinition,

[9] See above, pp. 59 f.
[1] See above, pp. 43 f.

serves as the contrasting background for the transition to the "second phase" of socialism. The crisis provides the favorable international environment for concentrating domestic Soviet policy on this transition. In its discussion, there is a striking emphasis on the need for changes within the Soviet system—changes which are to transform the system itself into the "higher" second phase. A large part of Stalin's article is devoted to the refutation of the statements of those who maintain that under socialism (that is to say, in the present Soviet system) the correspondence between productive forces and production relations is such as to exclude contradictions. Against this view, Stalin maintains that there is no "full conformity" between the elements of the economic basis. The productive forces "run ahead" of the production relations also under socialism—this, according to Stalin, is the matrix of progress—and the production relations are bound to turn into a fetter of social development. However, while under conditions of private appropriation and control these contradictions must lead to a conflict which can be resolved only through an "explosion," under socialism, society is able to bring the lagging production relations into conformity with the character of the productive forces in good time and without "exploding" the social order. At a certain stage of the development, the growth of productivity will render possible a "distribution of labor among the branches of production . . . regulated not by the law of value . . . but by the growth of society's need for goods." [2] This is the basic feature of the "second phase of socialism" ("communism"). Stalin

---

[2] "Economic Problems of Socialism," in *Current Soviet Policies,* p. 5. The contradictions existing in socialist society are again emphasized in Khrushchev's speech of November 6, 1957 (as broadcast by Moscow Home Service, p. A-23).

refers to Engels: "Socially planned regulation of production in accordance with the needs both of society
as a whole *and of each individual.*" [3] The underscored
words in the Engels quotation (which did not occur
in Stalin's own formulation above) are decisive: they
preclude the authoritarian identification of *society's*
need for goods with the needs of all its *individual
members.* According to Marx and Engels, communism prevails only if and when society's needs are
really the individual needs, and when their development and satisfaction determines the social division
of labor. But nothing in Stalin's own characterization
of the second phase suggests the abandonment of the
administrative authoritarian identification of society's
needs with those of its members. According to his
conception, since the growth of the productive forces
is no longer counteracted by antagonistic private
interests, the adjustment of production relations to
this growth can be undertaken by the "directing
agencies" of the Soviet state.[4] The transition from
socialism to communism is *their* work; "communism"
will be introduced as an administrative measure.

As to the timing in terms of years, Soviet theo-
reticians still take as the basis the figure of three Five-
Year Plans, given by Stalin in his speech of February
9, 1946. Considering the adjustments that were made
recently, this would locate the transition to the second
phase between 1960 and 1965 at the latest.[5] More

[3] "Anti-Dühring," in *A Handbook of Marxism,* ed. by E.
Burns (New York, International Publishers, 1935), p. 294.
Italics added.

[4] "Economic Problems of Socialism," in *Current Soviet Policies,* p. 15.

[5] Ts. A. Stepanian, "Usloviia i puti perekhoda ot sotsializma
k kommunizmu" (The Conditions and the Paths of the
Transition from Socialism to Communism), in *O sovetskom
sotsialisticheskom obshchestve* (On Soviet Socialist Society),

important is the timing in terms of objective conditions. Stalin listed three "basic preliminary conditions": (1) Constant growth of all social production, with preponderant growth of the means of production," (2) the "raising of collective farm property to the level of property of the public as a whole," (3) "a cultural development of society as would ensure to all its members comprehensive development of their physical and mental abilities." [6] Stalin emphasized as the first necessary step for the attainment of the last condition the reduction of the working day "at least to six and then to five hours." As basic measures of economic policy during this period he considered the raising of real wages by at least 100 percent (through both an increase in money wages and a systematic reduction in prices of the goods of mass consumption),[7] and a gradual extension of the system of "product exchange" at the expense of the sphere of "commodity turnover" (especially by including the surplus collective-farm production in the sphere of product exchange).[8]

This outline of the transition to the second phase reiterates the traditional Marxist conception, derived chiefly from Engèls's remarks in the third part of *Anti-Dühring*. But within the context of Stalin's statement, the standard propositions obtained the weight of a policy directive and were as such accepted by Stalin's anti-Stalinist successors.

The first fact to be noted is that the present post-Stalinist and anti-Stalinist trend continues the main

ed. by F. Konstantinov (Moscow, Gospolitizdat, 1948), pp. 540-42.
[6] Stalin, "Economic Problems of Socialism," in *Current Soviet Policies,* pp. 14 f.
[7] *Ibid.,* p. 14.
[8] *Ibid.,* p. 19.

line of late Stalinist policy with respect to the problems of "transition." We have tried to show this in
the case of the evaluation of capitalist development.[9]
The same holds true with regard to the principal
objectives of Soviet policy. The resolution adopted
by the Twentieth Congress reasserts "the main economic task," namely, "to catch up with and to outstrip
the most developed capitalist countries in production
per capita." For the attainment of the goals, the
Resolution reasserts the priority of heavy industry,
together with a need for "rapid development" in the
production of consumer goods. Like Stalin, Khrushchev
rejected "utopian views" of the transition. Following
Stalin's statement of the "basic preliminary conditions"
for progress, the Resolution provides for the reduction
of the working day in the course of the Sixth Five-
Year Plan to seven hours for all workers and to six
hours for those in the coal- and ore-mining industries.
The same consistency prevails in the emphasis on
technological education, the training of "specialists,"
and the "ties of the country's scientific establishments
with production."[1]

The continuity between Stalinism and post-Stalinism
might still be that of basic propaganda requirements,
were it not for the possibility that it may reflect a
dynamic inherent in the Soviet social system itself.

We have proposed that the Soviet construction of
socialism, while progressing, develops a dialectic of
its own. On the one hand, the totalitarian administration strengthens itself *and* the very forces against
which it acts (thereby creating a stronger consolidation of Western society); in doing so, it perpetuates

[9] See above, pp. 49 ff.
[1] *XX S"ezd Kommunisticheskoi Partii Sovetskogo Soiuza*
(The Twentieth Congress of the Communist Party of the Soviet
Union), II, 434, 475, 480.

he repressive economic and political features of the
Soviet system. On the other hand, the administration
depends, for the attainment of its main objective ("to
catch up with and outstrip") on the all-out development of the productive forces at its disposal. This
development—under the impact of an international
competition which Soviet Marxism regards as a
struggle for survival—drives the growing productivity, with the most streamlined weapons of modern
technology and science, toward a level at which it
will tend to "overflow" into production for individual
needs. Given conditions under which the growing
production can be sustained at full capacity, and
under which this capacity is not to an increasing
degree utilized for wasteful and destructive purposes,
production is likely to generate the material and cultural wealth that would permit the stipulated features
of the second phase. (They are modest enough.) This
seems to be the case even if in their development the
productive forces also sustain a large and greatly
privileged bureaucracy. Productivity may be expected
to run ahead of privileges and effectuate a gradual
but qualitative change in the circumstances of the
underprivileged population and, correspondingly, in
the political institutions—as it did at preceding stages
of an expanding civilization.

The totalitarian administration has, of course, sufficient power to counteract this trend, and it must be
expected to do so if the administration operates under
an interest antagonistic to the growth of productivity
and its use for the satisfaction of individual needs, or
if it considers counteraction necessary for the existence
of the Soviet state. We have tried to show[2] that the
first condition does not prevail. The "class interest" of

[2] Pages 99 ff. above.

the bureaucracy (that is, the common denominator of
the special interests of the various branches of the
bureaucracy) is linked to the intensified development
of the productive forces, and administrative progress
into a "higher stage of socialism" would most effec
tively secure the cohesion of Soviet society. On the
other hand, the Soviet state has consistently diverted a
very large sector of the productive forces (human and
material) to the business of external and interna
militarization. Does this policy forestall the transition
to the "second phase"? The compatibility of an armament economy with a rising standard of living is more
than a technical economic problem. The maintenance
of a vast military establishment (armed forces and
secret police) with its educational, political and psy
chological controls perpetuates authoritarian institu
tions, attitudes, and behavior patterns which counter
act a qualitative change in the repressive production
relations. Inasmuch as the bureaucracy is a separate
class with special privileges and powers, it has an
interest in self-perpetuation and, consequently, in
perpetuating repressive production (and political) re
lations. However, the question is whether the repres
sive economic and political relations on which this
bureaucracy was founded are not increasingly con
tradicting the more fundamental and general interests
and objectives in the development of the Soviet
state.

If our analysis of Soviet Marxism is correct, the
answer must be affirmative. The fundamental Soviet
objective in the present period is the breaking of the
consolidation of the Western world which neutralizes
the "interimperialist conflicts" on whose effectiveness
the final victory of socialism depends. The same forces
which make for and preserve this consolidation also

endanger and delay the attainment of the goal "to catch up with and surpass" the capabilities of advanced capitalism. In the Soviet Marxist analysis, Western consolidation is based on a "permanent war economy," which, taking advantage of the head start of capitalism, sustains the rapid development of productivity in the capitalist countries and the integration of the majority of organized labor within the capitalist system. Thus it continues to delay the revolution in the capitalist world which even Stalin considered as ultimately indispensable for the triumph of socialism.[3] The capitalist war economy is in turn sustained by the "hard" Soviet policy, which also stands in the way of Soviet progress to the second phase where it can effectively compete with capitalist capabilities. Consequently, the first step must be the relaxation of the "hard" policy. This, however, is a matter of internal as well as foreign reorientation, of shifting the emphasis from military and political to more effective economic competition, and of liberalizing the Stalinist bureaucracy. The shift presupposes a high level of industrialization. Soviet success in the utilization of atomic energy may have been one of the significant events which has convinced the Soviet leadership that the adequate competitive level of industrialization has been reached.

We believe that these factors are behind recent Soviet developments. If this is the case, the shift is part of a long-range trend, originating in an objective historical situation and pertaining to the very structure

[3] Soviet Marxism considers the socio-economic rather than the military potentialities of the international constellation: the internal strength of Western society, most conspicuously expressed in the higher standard of living and in "class collaboration" is, in Marxian terms, a greater long-range threat to the "final victory of socialism" than is Western military power.

of Soviet society. The objective historical situation (i.e., the interrelation between Stalinist power politics and capitalist consolidation) drove the Soviet state to a reconsideration of its basic strategy, a "relaxation" which, if successful, tends toward an increasing use of the growing productivity for consumers' needs. The basic economic trend would generate a corresponding political trend, that is, liberalization of the repressive totalitarian regime.

In Soviet policy toward the Western world, evidence for the new trend had been cumulative from the end of the Korean war to the upheavals in Eastern Europe in 1956. Corresponding developments had also taken place in intercommunist relations: the Soviet-Yugoslav *rapprochement;* the commitment of the Indian and the Japanese parties to a "legal-democratic" program; continuation (and even intensification) of the "soft" strategy of the Western Communist parties, especially of the united front policy—de-Stalinization. It was this de-Stalinization which stimulated the events in Poland and Hungary. The Soviet leadership reacted in accordance with the underlying policy conception. Soviet Marxism has never acknowledged a genuine third alternative to socialism or capitalism, and the former is defined, for the period of coexistence, in terms of a firm alliance with the Soviet Union. A break in the "protective belt" of Eastern European states is, in the Soviet interpretation, therefore tantamount to an ascent of capitalist influence and to a change of the international balance of power at a vital point in favor of the capitalist world. Moreover, while the liberalization in the Soviet Union rested on a firm basis of industrialization and collectivization, this was not the case in the Eastern European countries. Industrialization was still at a very backward stage, and the peasantry was not yet effectively coordinated with the nationalized economy and its political institutions. The movement toward "national communism" was therefore considered as objectively premature and anti-socialist regardless of the sincere subjective intentions of the national leadership and their followers among the working classes and the intelligentsia.

The Eastern European events were likely to slow down and perhaps even reverse de-Stalinization in some fields; particularly in international strategy, a considerable "hardening" has become apparent. However, if our analysis is correct, the fundamental trend will continue and reassert itself throughout such reversals. With respect to internal Soviet developments, this means at present continuation of "collective leadership," decline in the power of the secret police, decentralization, legal reforms, relaxation in censorship, liberalization in cultural life. The relation of this policy to the long-range socio-economic trend may be illustrated by the continued preferential development of heavy industry as against the development of consumers' goods industries. The "Malenkov line" interpreted Stalin's statement on the prevailing conflict between productive forces and production relations as necessitating a change in the relation between the two main divisions of production in favor of the second division, namely, that of consumers' goods industries[4] —in spite of Stalin's injunction that the "predominant growth" of the first division must remain the basis of socialist planning. Although the theory of shifting the

[4] See for example A. N. Maslin, "Printsip material'noi zainteresovannosti pri sotsializme" (The Principle of Material Interest under Socialism), *Voprosy Filosofii* (Problems of Philosophy), 1954, No. 4, pp. 3-14; 1955, No. 1, p. 15.

priority to the second division was not officially rejected until January, 1955, opposition to it was already
outspoken in 1954 under the Malenkov regime:

There must be no place in Soviet science for discussion
with vulgarizers and falsifiers of Marxism. Some economists
. . . attempted to revise one of the fundamental principles
of economic teaching of Marxism, i.e., the thesis that enlarged reproduction, especially under socialism, requires
preferential development of Subdivision I (production of
means of production) as against Subdivision II (production of means of consumption).[5]

Distorting the substance of the action carried out by the
party and the Soviet government steeply to raise agriculture
and increase production of products for popular consumption, some economists started asserting that under socialism
enlarged reproduction to become effective does not necessarily require a more rapid development of the production
of the means of production as compared to production of
consumers' goods.[6]

Priority for the development of heavy industry is
considered essential for the transition to communism
not only in terms of the internal growth of the social
product but also in terms of the international implications—in other words, the military as well as economic
position of the USSR must be strengthened:

Having fulfilled the industrialization program devised by
the party in the prewar Five-Year Plans, the Soviet people
established a solid economic basis for an active defense of
the country. A mighty heavy industry proved the foundation of the USSR's indestructible defensive power.[7]

[5] M. T. Iovchuk, "Rol' sotsialisticheskoi ideologii v bor'be
s perezhitkami kapitalizma" (The Role of Socialist Ideology
in the Struggle with Survivals of Capitalism), *Voprosy Filosofii*
(Problems of Philosophy), 1955, No. 1, p. 15.
[6] I. Doroshev and A. Rumiantsev, "Protiv izvrashcheniia
marksistskoi teorii vosproizvodstva" (Against the Distortion
of the Marxist Theory of Reproduction), *Kommunist* (Communist), 1955, No. 2 (January), p. 14.
[7] E. Frolov, "Tiazhelaia industriia—osnova ekonomicheskogo
mogushchestva SSSR" (Heavy Industry—The Basis of the

Under the conditions of coexistence with the capitalist
world, the party and the government are thus committed to maintain the policy of preferential development of heavy industry for the communist as well as
socialist construction of Soviet society.

To be sure, behind the doctrinal controversy probably lies a struggle between the top bureaucracies for
their share in power. Unquestionably, a decisive shift
in production priority would involve a corresponding
shift in political weight: the influence of the managerial strata in heavy industry would be bound to
decline. However, the political struggle has a more
basic content; Soviet society seems to have reached
another turning point in its development. The Soviet
leadership itself has defined this turning point: a level
of growth has been reached where progress no longer
requires the alternative of either increasing heavy
industry *or* the standard of living, but where the latter
can be achieved as a result of the former. Reduced to
its fundamental contention, the idea now is: not competitive preparedness for war *or* competitive satisfaction of popular needs, but *both*. The alternative was
that of the Stalinist era; it is now held surpassed by
the success of this era.

On this Malenkov and his opponents seem to have
been in agreement. When Molotov was called upon in
October, 1955, to retract his "erroneous" statement (of
February, 1955) that merely the "foundations" of a socialist society had been laid, and instead to confirm
that a socialist society itself had been built, he was
called upon to acknowledge the completion of a whole
period (with which he himself has been identified) and

Economic Might of the USSR), *Kommunist* (Communist),
1955, No. 3 (February), pp. 29 f. See also the second editorial
in the same number, p. 22.

the beginning of a new one. But it was Khrushche
who stated most succinctly the socio-economic reasor
for the superseding of the Stalinist alternative. In h
report on the agricultural program, delivered in Se
tember, 1953, he said:

> The Communist Party has steadily maintained a cours
> of overall development in heavy industry as essential
> the successful development of all branches of the nation
> economy, and it has achieved great success on this roa
> Chief attention was turned to solving this immediate n
> tional economic problem, and basic forces and means we
> diverted to it. Our best cadres were occupied with th
> work of industrializing the country. We did not have th
> means for high-speed, simultaneous development of heav
> industry, agriculture, and light industry. For this it w
> necessary to provide needed prerequisites. *Now these pr*
> *requisites exist.* We have a mighty industrial base, strength
> ened collective farms and cadres trained in all branches
> economic construction.[8]

This is the internal reason for the new trend: th
Leninist program of "civilization" [9] has been fulfilled i
the first phase; through the Stalinist construction, a
industrial base has been created sufficiently strong t
meet international "emergencies" and to raise the cor
sumption level in the USSR. What could not hav
been done "simultaneously" before can now be under
taken: the "forced development" of heavy industr
can continue while allowing an increasing proportio
of the social product to flow into the satisfaction
individual consumers' needs.

But if the decision to accelerate and enlarge th
production of consumer goods while continuing th
preferential development of heavy industry indicat
the measure of progress beyond the Stalinist perio

[8] *Current Digest of the Soviet Press,* V. No. 39 (Novemb
7, 1953), 11 f.
[9] See pp. 30 f. above.

also indicates that progress will be kept within the amework of "nonantagonistic" contradictions and administrative adjustments. In other words, any expectation of a qualitative change which would amount to a explosive "negation" of the past stage is rigidly opposed. Improvement and liberalization will be conditional upon the relentless struggle for higher productivity of labor, upon socialist competition, and upon total mobilization of the people for work and r training. Again, such continuity in the "spirit" of socialism cannot simply be explained by the "power ive" of the Soviet leadership—it is rather rooted in the objective conditions under which the Soviet state operates, in the "anomaly" of capitalist and socialist coexistence which Lenin's political testament epitomized. The notion of socialism in a "capitalist environment" precludes abandonment of the total mobilization the people; it also precludes a fundamental change the value system which subordinates socialist freedom to toil and discipline. It is the Soviet government and the party which will raise the level of popular consumption. This constantly repeated formula expresses the basic policy that progress and liberalization, the effect of the "basic law of socialism," will not the result of freedom and initiative "from below" but rather of the utilization of an expanding economy, regulated by the state in accordance with the political requirements (national and international). The resolution to maintain this policy is demonstrated by the manner in which political and cultural liberalization remains fused with improvement in a repressive morality, private and public, in work and in leisure.

We shall analyze the social function of Soviet morality in the second part of this study. Here, the question arises whether the "spirit" of socialist con-

struction as institutionalized during the Stalinist peri
will also be fundamentally affected by the new tren
Even a most tentative answer would have to discu
two chief factors: the attained stage of the economi
political development, and the inner dynamic of tl
established behavior pattern and value system, whic
though planned and controlled, have their own ex
gencies and aims. Only a tentative answer with respe
to the economic-political factor can be sketched
this point.

We have seen that, in the Stalinist conception, tl
disappearance of the state as repressive machinery
made conditional on the strengthening of the sociali
state, and that the latter is to continue into the secon
phase. There are no indications that this concepti
has been altered since Stalin's death. Although Stalir
"erroneous formula" on the aggravating class strugg
during the progress of socialism is rejected,[1] althou
a considerable "democratization" of the state, dece
tralization, and self-government is proclaimed ar
even implemented, the continued strengthening
the state and of the party agencies remains on tl
agenda.[2] Nor—and this is far more important—a
there any objective factors or tendencies which wou
allow such alteration. The reorientation in internation
strategy, and the corresponding domestic reorient
tion, especially in the field of agriculture, confront tl
regime with problems of such a magnitude that i

[1] Resolution of the Central Committee of the Commun
Party of the Soviet Union, June 30, 1956, in *The Anti-Sta*
Campaign and International Communism, ed. by Russian Ins
tute, Columbia University (New York, Columbia Universi
Press, 1956), p. 290.
[2] Khrushchev at the Twentieth Congress of the Commun
Party of the Soviet Union, *XX S"ezd Kommunisticheš*
Partii Sovetskogo Soiuza (The Twentieth Congress of t
Communist Party of the Soviet Union), I, 91 ff.

tense regimentation from above seems to be required for the very success of the new efforts. Relaxation no less than hardening of the system necessitates planned control. The gulf, in terms of privileges and of power, between the bureaucracy and the underlying population is still great enough to make for the self-perpetuation of the former. Moreover, education and training of the people are geared to a well-functioning mass of competitive subjects of administration. According to the doctrine itself, the very nature of the state as an independent power over and above the individuals must sustain the separation of the "immediate producers" from control over the means of production: social unfreedom reproduces political unfreedom. The trend we have suggested is toward alleviating the latter; but only if it affects the former, or, in Stalin's terminology, only if the contradictions between the growing productive forces and the production relations have really been solved, would the entire structure change. This solution is reserved for the "final victory of socialism," and the "final" victory of socialism is still linked to the international revolution. In this respect, the initiative in the turn toward the "withering away" of the state is not with the Soviet leadership—the turn depends on the break in the "capitalist environment" and its effects on Soviet society.

The sustained power of the state sustains the controls over the ideological sphere. The relaxation might be considerable; individual liberties are likely to increase with increasing economic benefits—but quantity will not turn into quality unless the economic benefits have themselves become political ones, that is to say, have led to the control of production by the "immediate producers," or, according to the progress of automation, by the "immediate consumers." As long

as this is not the case, the post-Stalinist welfare state
will remain the direct heir of the Stalinist state. And
for just as long, the basic "spirit" of socialism will remain the same. Soviet society in this case pays tribute
to the dialectic of ideology and reality, consciousness
and societal relations. According to this dialectic, a
genuinely socialist base is reflected in an ideology
which is *free* in a strict sense. The mental development in all its manifestations is freed from the blind
determination by the "realm of necessity" and tends
toward a free play of humane individual faculties.
Materialism is canceled through its realization; as
the economy is brought under the control of the associated individuals whose material needs are fulfilled,
their mental development is released from control. The
rational regulation of the necessities, of the struggle for
existence and the struggle with nature, enables society
to dispense with the regulation of the instinctual and
intellectual life of its members. Reason appears as
individual freedom. In Soviet society, however, the
progressing control of the base continues to be accompanied by a progressing control of the ideology, and
by the regulation of the realm of freedom gained by
conquest of the necessity. In the very passage where
Stalin calls for the reduction of the working day "at
least to six and then to five hours" (a measure in which
Marx saw the basic prerequisite for freedom), he
states that this reduction is necessary "in order that
members of society may receive the leisure time necessary for a thorough education." Thus the time saved
will not be *free* time—it will have to be spent in
education.

To be sure, education is the prerequisite for liberation: only the freedom to learn and to know the whole
truth, to grasp the arrested, violated, and destroyed

potentialities of man and nature can guide the building
of a free society. What kind of education did Stalin
envisage? He demanded the introduction of "universal,
compulsory, polytechnical education, so that a member of society may be able to make a free choice of
occupation and not be shackled for life to any one
occupation." [3] Following up this program, the Twentieth Congress again places all emphasis on "training"
—the training of "specialists on the basis of a close
cooperation between studies and production" and calls
for "strengthening the ties of the country's scientific
establishments with production, with the concrete demands of the national economy." [4] The exchangeability
of functions, the elimination of the institutionalized
division of labor,[5] is indeed in Marxian theory the characteristic of a socialist society—as a precondition for
the all-sided development of the genuinely human
faculties *outside* the process of material production.
But in Stalin's context the Marxian idea appears as
that of a society in which all men are technicians and
engineers. For Marx and Engels, the goal of communism was the "abolition of labor," [6] in the Soviet
Marxist conception, all will be laborers of the one
communist society.[7] With the free time transformed

[3] "Economic Problems of Socialism," in *Current Soviet
Policies*, p. 14.
[4] Resolution as broadcast by Tass, February 25, 1956; *XX
S"ezd Kommunisticheskoi Partii Sovetskogo Soiuza* (The
Twentieth Congress of the Communist Party of the Soviet
Union), II, 480.
[5] *Not* the division of labor as such—only that mode of
division which chains the laborer for life to one specialized
performance and function.
[6] Marx and Engels, *The German Ideology* (New York, International Publishers, 1939), pp. 49, 69.
[7] Stepanian, "Usloviia i puti perekhoda ot sotsializma k
kommunizmu" (The Conditions and the Paths of the Transition from Socialism to Communism), in *O sovetskom sotsialisticheskom obshchestve* (On Soviet Socialist Society), pp.
486 f.

into education time for polytechnical training, with the work morale anchored in the instinctual structure of man, administrative control is secured, and the past is safely transferred into the future. Stalin could thus quote without danger Engels's statement that labor will change from a burden into enjoyment. The enjoyment, however, will not be qualitatively different from that permitted under repression.

The ideological perspective parallels the political perspective. The state will continue into the period of communism—as will the "capitalist environment." For the state is the "collective subject" of the national economy which organizes the whole of society, and this organization has become the objectified representative of society over and above the individuals. Since societal production is systematically directed by the state and since the basic decisions are imposed upon the society by the state, progress itself, that is to say, the use of the growing productivity for the needs and aspirations of the individuals, must pass through the agencies of the state. The continuity of the administration thus bridges the gap between necessity and freedom, and assimilates the first and the second phase, socialism and communism. And the administration, as we have tried to show, depends on the ever more effective growth and utilization of the productivity of labor: it tends to drive society to a higher stage. Industrialization and rationalization, carried through according to standards of competitive efficiency at the national and international level, and developing human beings as ever better functioning instruments of material and intellectual labor, are likely to bear economic as well as political fruits—overruling the diverging interests and intentions of particular groups and individuals.

The reward will not be the end of domination of man by man; administration of things is not likely to replace the administration of men in any foreseeable future. Marx stressed the essentially "neutral" character of technology: although the windmill may give you a feudal society, and the steammill an industrial capitalist society, the latter may just as well give you another form of industrial society. Modern machinery is susceptible to capitalist as well as socialist utilization. This amounts to saying that mature capitalism and socialism have the same *technical* base, and that the historical decision as to how this base is to be used is a *political* decision. During the period of co-existence, the economic factors are political factors; it is the period of political economy with respect not only to the state's role in the economy, but also to the political implications of the development of consciousness. The consciousness of the underlying population, permeated with the power of ever growing productivity, with the efficiency of an ever better mechanized and coordinated apparatus, and with the rewards of an ever more indispensable compliance, does not attain any other political level than that of the apparatus itself. Thus it is barred from developing the political consciousness which may serve as a guide to political change.

The two antagonistic social systems here join in the general trend of technical progress. It has been noted (and we shall attempt to demonstrate this notion by the example of Soviet ethical philosophy in the second part of this study) how much the present "communist spirit" resembles the "capitalist spirit" which Max Weber attributed to the rising capitalist civilization. The Soviet state seems to foster the disciplining, self-propelling, competitive-productive elements of this

spirit in a streamlined and politically controlled form.
"Businesslike management," directorial initiative and
responsibility, and scientific rationalization of the
human and material resources have remained the consistently imposed demands throughout both the Stalinist and post-Stalinist period,[8] in times of both "hard"
and "soft" policy, of both personal and collective
leadership. And "businesslike management" has also
been applied to grand international strategy, to the
conduct of foreign affairs. The change in the type of
leader, from the professional revolutionary to the
manager (a change which began as early as 1922
with the development of the New Economic Policy)
now seems to be consummated. In 1922 Lenin proclaimed preference for the merchant, the trader, the
administrator over the loyal revolutionary communist
who did not know how to trade, how to sell, how to
do business. He went further than that: "We are not
afraid to say that the character of our work has
changed. Our worst internal enemy is the Communist
who occupies a responsible (or not responsible) Soviet
post and enjoys universal respect as a conscientious
man." [9]

However, the spirit of businesslike politics and competitive efficiency in the twentieth century is no longer
that described by Max Weber. Developed industrial
society requires a different organization and a different
behavior. Soviet society, in the position of a "late

[8] See for example Bulganin's report to the Central Committee of the Communist Party, July, 1955, in Current Digest
of the Soviet Press, VII, 28 (August 24, 1955), 3-20, and
Zverev's speech at the session of the Supreme Soviet, February, 1955, in ibid., VII, No. 6 (March 23, 1955), 19-20
and No. 7 (March 30, 1955), 8.
[9] "Report at the All-Russian Congress of the Metal Workers'
Union," in Selected Works (12 vols.; New York, International
Publishers, 1937-38), IX, 318, see also p. 326.

omer" telescoping entire phases of growth, meets its
antagonist in a common situation. At the "atomic" stage
of the mastery of man and nature, societal productivity
surpasses the traditional forms of control and utilization. The cohesion of society is no longer left to the
free play of economic forces and their individual
evaluation and calculation; they have to be supplemented by more powerful regulation. The fusion between economic, cultural, and political controls is an
international phenomenon, cutting across differences
in economic, cultural, and political institutions. In the
Soviet Union, this fusion is an avowed ideological as
well as economic goal: at the very time when Soviet
industry is again to be revamped in accordance with
the standards of business efficiency, the government
emphasized that this program is to be implemented
by strengthening the "industrial leadership" of the
Communist Party! [1]

There is no prospect that this fusion of economic
and political controls in a self-perpetuating state will
dissolve; it is doubly grounded, in the nationalized but
not socialized Soviet economy, and in the international
situation of large-scale industry. This framework of
the state leaves room for many changes within the
administration: the top rule may pass from one group
to the other, from party to army predominance, from
"committee rule" back to personal rule, and so forth.
However, these changes would not fundamentally alter
the basis of Soviet society, nor the basic direction in
which this society is moving. Unless another world war
or similar catastrophe occurs which would change the
situation, the direction is toward a growing welfare

---

[1] See Bulganin's report to the Central Committee of the
Communist Party, July, 1955, in *Current Digest of the Soviet
Press*, VII, No. 28 (August 24, 1955), 18 ff.

state. Rising standards of living up to a practically free
distribution of basic goods and services, steadily ex
tending mechanization of labor, exchangeability o
technical functions, expanding popular culture—thes
developments constitute the probable trend. It is likel
to lead to the gradual assimilation of urban an
agricultural, intellectual and physical labor—brough
under the common denominator of technology. Tech
nical progress will overtake the repressive restriction
imposed at earlier stages—they will become technicall
obsolete. This will lead to further changes in the polit
ical structure: it will make for a spread of the bureauc
racy and its privileges, for a reduction of the ga
between the top strata and the underlying population
for the transformation of political into technologica
controls. Personal rule will increasingly be replace
by collective administration, even if a new dictato
should concentrate the leadership at the top. Socia
mobility within the system will grow. But thes
changes themselves will take place within the frame
work of universal control, universal administratio
Whether or not the growth of the welfare state wil
ultimately bring the administration under direct popu
lar control, that is to say, whether or not the Sovie
state will develop into a socialist or communist demo
racy, is a question for which the prevailing facts an
tendencies do not provide a workable hypothesi
Negatively, it seems that nothing in the structure
Soviet society would exclude such a long-range de
velopment, and that it would depend neither on
"decision" of the Soviet leadership nor on the intern
situation of the Soviet orbit alone. From our analysi
it follows that the emergence of a socialist democra
in the USSR would be conditional upon two main pre
requisites, which in turn are interrelated: (1) a leve

of social wealth which would make possible the organization of production according to individual needs and thus cancel the prerogatives of privileged powers; and (2) an international situation in which the conflict between the two social systems would no longer define their economy and their policy.

We have suggested that such qualitative change is no longer an economic but a political problem:[2] the technical-economic basis for the change is there. It is not the still terrifying scarcity and poverty which prevents "socialist democracy," that is, the control of production and distribution "from below." In Marxist terms, distribution of scarcity and the concerted struggle for its abolition pertain to the content of socialism from the very beginning—even during the first phase.[3] On the basis of the nationalized economy, establishment of this control remains a political act. As such, it involves the abolition of the repressive state and its repressive machinery—which does not necessarily mean violent overthrow in civil war. However, the political act itself seems to be dependent on the second prerequisite. The rising welfare state may render life more comfortable and more secure, but as long as the East-West conflict remains a determining economic and political factor, it precludes the decisive transformation, for it serves to justify—subjectively and objectively—repressive competition and competitive mobilization on a totalitarian scale. The history of Soviet society seems to be fatefully linked to that of its antagonist. Over and above the construction of socialism or communism in one country and in one orbit, the essentially international element of socialism seems to prevail.

[2] Page 169 above.
[3] Page 6 above.

But in this constellation, the prospective development of the Soviet state stands under the dialectical law which it invokes. The qualitative change can never be envisaged as an automatic one. No matter how high the level of technical progress and material culture, of labor productivity and efficiency, the change from socialist necessity to socialist freedom can only be the result of conscious effort and decision. The maintenance of repressive production relations enables the Soviet state, with the instrumentalities of universal control, to regiment the consciousness of the underlying population. We have suggested that the bureaucracy may not have a vested interest in perpetuating the repressive state machinery.[4] However, this does not dispose of the question as to whether or not the "spirit" of Soviet socialist construction, the specific "rationality" of the system, tends to perpetuate repression by and in the underlying population itself—in other words, whether repression from above does not meet repression from below. The Soviet system would then repeat and reproduce that determinism which Marx attributed to the basic processes of capitalist society. There, Marxian theory and practice themselves were to be the lever which would break this determinism and free the subjective factor, that is, the class consciousness of the proletariat. We have tried to show that, in Soviet society, Marxism no longer has this function. Left without a conceptual level for the "determinate negation" of the established system, for comprehending and realizing its arrested potentialities, the ruled tend not only to submit to the rulers but also to reproduce in themselves their subordination. Again, this process is not specific to Soviet society. The means and rewards of highly advanced industrial

[4] See pp. 93 ff. above.

society, the work and leisure attitudes called forth by its organization of production and distribution, establish a human existence which makes for a change in basic values—for a transformation of freedom into security. Such a transformation in turn would counteract the development of a "negative" political consciousness and thus counteract qualitative political change. The basic value system, the prevalent "spirit" of the society, would then assume the role of an active factor determining the direction of the societal development. As a partial contribution to the analysis of this factor, the second part of this study will examine the main structure of Soviet ethical philosophy.

PART · II

Ethical Tenets

9

WESTERN AND SOVIET ETHICS: THEIR HISTORICAL RELATION

In the first part of this study we have analyzed certain basic trends of Soviet Marxism in their relation to the development of Soviet society. The analysis led to the conclusion that the specific conditions and objectives of industrialization, carried out in antagonistic competition with the Western world, determined even the most theoretical features of Soviet Marxism. At the same time, it appeared that in some significant aspects the two antagonistic systems showed a parallel tendency: total industrialization seemed to exact patterns of attitude and organization which cut across the essential political and ideological differences. Efficient, "businesslike management," highly rationalized and centralized, and working on equally rationalized and coordinated human and technical material, tends to promote political and cultural centralization and coordination. In the West, this trend has led to a corrosion of the humanistic liberal ethics which was centered on the idea of the autonomous individual and his inalienable rights. But the system of values derived from an earlier stage has by and large been maintained (after the liquidation of the Fascist and Nazi states which subverted it)—though in increasingly overt contradiction to the prevailing practice. In the Soviet state, total industrialization occurred under conditions incompatible with liberal ethics; therefore, the revolutionary and postrevolutionary state created its own system of values and indoctrinated the population accordingly. However, contemporary total industrialization with contemporary technics and methods of work provide a common denominator which makes the abstract contrast between Western and Soviet ethics questionable.

Neither centralization nor coordination militate by themselves against progress in freedom and humanity (they have more than once been effective weapons in the struggle against oppression and reaction). Nor is there anything in the technics and economics of total industrialization that would necessarily encroach upon human freedom. On the contrary, if there is anything common to the Marxian and anti-Marxian evaluation of industrial society in nineteenth-century philosophy, it is the insistence that increasing industrialization is the prerequisite for progress in the ethical as well as the material sense. The protest against the "alienation" of man, which materialist and idealist philosophy express, is in both cases directed against the *political organization*[1] of industry—not against industry as such. In Marxian (but certainly not in Soviet-Marxist) terms it

---

[1] "Political" as distinguished from "social" refers to an organization and utilization of industry which is not determined by the faculties and needs of the individuals but by particular interests conflicting with the free development of individual faculties and needs. Under this condition too, production fulfills a "social need," but the latter is superimposed upon the individual needs and shapes them in accordance with the predominant specific interests.

would be easy to identify the common element in the
political organization of industry which militates
against progress in freedom, namely, the enslavement
of man by the means of his labor, his subordination to
his own "objectified" (*vergegenständlichte*) labor. Still,
in history, such subordination had very different functions: it may initiate a new stage in the development
of the productive forces or prolong an old one; it may
promote or arrest the development. The political organization of industry can by itself not explain the
specific content of Soviet ethics and its relation to
Western ethics.

We propose to approach the problem through a
brief comparison between the representative ideas of
Western and Soviet ethics. Such a comparison assumes
that there is on both sides an identifiable body of
ethical theory sufficiently homogeneous to be treated
as a whole. The assumption seems plausible in the
case of Soviet ethics: throughout all changes to which
Soviet ethical theories have been subjected since the
Bolshevik Revolution, they have been governed by
one unifying principle, namely, the formulation and
evaluation of ethical standards in accordance with
the objectives of the Soviet state. And in so far as these
objectives themselves have been determined by the
long-range policy of socialism under conditions of
coexistence,[2] a striking continuity and consistency
have been preserved notwithstanding all adaptations
to the changing situation. But can a similar case be
made for the contrasting homogeneity of Western
ethics? The case seems to be legitimate *a contrario*.
If we look at the ethical standards and ideas on which
the Soviet discussion of Western ethics is centered
and which are criticized and reinterpreted, we dis-

[2] See Chapter 4 of this study.

cover certain general features which appear as characteristic of Western ethics. They are as follows:

1. The notion of freedom obtains; according to this the essential condition of man is that he be sufficiently *free from* external determination to become *free for* self-responsible action and behavior.

2. This essential freedom validates the proposition of *universally binding ethical norms,* to be observed regardless of the individual's accidental situation and objectives.

3. The ethically legitimate aims of the individual are those which involve the best possible development and satisfaction of his faculties, but individual self-realization is subordinated to (*a*) the universally valid norms of Christian ethics and their humanistic secularization; (*b*) the more specific norms of the social and political community in which the individual lives.

4. The two sets of norms are sanctioned (*a*) by God and/or "the nature of man"; and (*b*) by the requirements of sustaining and improving the social and national community.

5. But regardless of the ultimate sanction of morality, the supposition is that there is no *fundamental* conflict[3] between individual morality on the one hand, and communal (social and political) morality on the other; that is to say, in the countries of Western (industrial) civilization, the basic social and political relations are held to be organized in such a way that the objectives of the individual (Point 3 above) and his "essence" (Points 1-2 above) can be attained or at least reasonably aspired to *within* the institutions

---

[3] Although there certainly is (and ought to be) factual tension and difference.

of the established society. These institutions can and must be improved, and their improvement may even imply large-scale changes; however, such changes are generally envisaged, not as the negation of the established society but as its expansion and growth.

The last proposition states the hidden *historical* denominator of Western ethics: it presupposes that civilization has finally established the institutions and relationships within whose framework man can realize his "nature," that is to say, unfold his potentialities and fulfill his needs. This presupposition is common to both idealistic and pragmatist-positivistic ethics, to the theories expounded by the French rationalists, the English utilitarians, the German idealists, and by Saint-Simon and his followers. But the political and industrial revolutions of the eighteenth and nineteenth centuries are not its only source. Its moral substance is deeply rooted in the Christian tradition. Ever since Christian ethics ceased to be an "oppositional" ethics, since its adoption by the state, the representative ethical philosophies have condemned as heresy a morality which maintained that the established civilization was in *irreconcilable* conflict with the potentialities of man. To be sure, man's salvation and redemption are not of this world; but this world does not only not preclude his salvation, his moral behavior in it is also a necessary precondition for his salvation.[4] All philosophy which does not accept this presupposition is, from the point of view of representative Western ethics, in a strict sense not only *heretic* but also *amoral* if not *immoral*. For such nonaccept-

---

[4] Calvinist doctrine is no exception. "Good works" and merits are not identical with moral behavior in the Christian sense.

ance implies rejection of the fundamental assumption
on which the universal validity of the moral principles
rests, namely, the possibility of their realization.

However, the "heretic" philosophies have survived
in many forms—from the Gnostic schools of the first
Christian centuries, the Cathari and other radical
spiritual sects, to the revolutionary social philosophies
of the modern era. Common to all of them is their
commitment to a qualitatively new history—a history
which must shatter the established institutions so that
the real destiny of man may be fulfilled. Common to
all of them is their attraction among the underprivileged and "marginal" strata of the population (and
their acceptance by various political and intellectual
"elites"). Their morality has a different historical
denominator and therefore appears as the negation
of the prevailing morality. But at the same time, the
heretics claim to preserve and even fulfill the principles
and promises maintained by their orthodox adver-
saries: the medieval Cathari claimed to be the true
Christians; the radical sects of the Reformation represented themselves as the true Protestants. During the
modern period, the opposition, increasingly secular,
continues within the humanist tradition. The great
materialists and skeptics of the sixteenth century, the
extreme left wing of the Enlightenment and its
socialist-communist heirs justify their "subversive"
philosophy in terms of the humanist ideal. Marxism
is an integral part of the same tradition. It was more
than a manner of speaking when Marx and Engels
considered themselves as heirs of the Enlightenment,
the French Revolution, and German idealistic philosophy. Liberty, Equality, and Justice are key terms in
Marx's *Capital*, and its economic theory is in a more
than chronological sense preceded by and completes

the humanist philosophy of the German Ideology (1860) and the Economic-Philosophical Manuscripts (1844).[5]

This outline, though oversimplified, may help to clarify the historical relation between Western and Soviet ethics. The main impact of Soviet ethical philosophy is not that of an external force operating from outside and against Western civilization. Nor does the challenge come from the specific content of Soviet ethics—from the ideals of "communist morality." Soviet ethics bases its claim to represent a "higher" morality on the historical mission of Marxian theory, and Marxian theory has no independent ethics but claims to demonstrate the *realization* of humanistic ethics. According to Marx, the capitalist economy is the fate and the denial of this code of ethics, and its abolition the prerequisite for the development of ethics. The historical roots of Soviet philosophy are not alien to the West (no matter how closely they have been fused with the Eastern tradition and adapted to the national and international interests of the Soviet Union). Nor are they primarily defined by the requirements of power and propaganda. They derive (1) from the revolutionary formulation of the humanist ideal in the theory of "scientific socialism," and (2) from its use for establishing a new society opposed to and competing with capitalist society. No matter how much the former contradicts the latter (the first part of this study tries to show how

[5] No complete English translation of the latter is available. The full text was first published in Division 1, Vol. III of the *Marx-Engels Gesamtausgabe* (Berlin, Marx-Engels Verlag, 1932). Also not available in English is Marx's *Grundrisse der Kritik der Politischen Oekonomie,* written 1857-58 (Berlin, Dietz, 1953). This is the most important of Marx's manuscripts, which shows to what extent the humanist philosophy is fulfilled and formulated in the economic theory of *Capital.*

much it does), the connection is close enough to
render possible the employment of the ideal in defense
of the reality. The forces and circumstances which
led to the abuse and violation of the ideal appear as
more objective than those of mere power politics—
objective to such an extent that they may easily be
presented as the working of Historical Reason. Within
this framework, Soviet ethical philosophy is an in-
ternally consistent, rational system of values, sufficiently separable from political expediencies to at-
tract the self-interest of large populations outside
the Soviet dominion.

This attraction seems to rest to a great extent on
an argument which implies that Marxism has rescued
humanistic ethics from capitalist distortion. It may be
summarized as follows:

The people in the Western world have been educated in the spirit of Christian-humanistic ethics. Their
societal relations are supposed to conform essentially
to this spirit and to render possible its ever more
adequate and universal realization—especially the
liberty and equality of man, and the development of
his human potentialities. Western civilization at its
industrial stage has indeed assembled all the material
and cultural resources necessary for implementing this
idea. However, the existing societal institutions prevent its implementation because they sustain injustice,
exploitation, and repression. Consequently, they must
be destroyed in order to fulfill the promises of Western
civilization.

This argument, which has been publicized in very
popular formulations and on various levels of sophisti-
cation, persuasion, and evidence, has had a lasting
influence. The mainsprings of this influence may be
defined as follows: The argument (1) derives the

pervasive discontent in civilization from one tangible and easily identifiable cause, namely, the capitalist organization of society; (2) it criticizes this society, not by any extraneous and transcendental standards, but by those promulgated and accepted by Western society (i.e., the "humanistic values"); (3) it thus explains and justifies discontent and protest not only on material but also on ethical grounds; (4) it offers an alternative which, again, is presented, not as an extraneous abstract possibility, but as the fulfillment of the very promises and capabilities of the existing society.

The last point indicates what seems to be the main force of the appeal—the combination of ethical maxims with scientific objectivity. Working with Marxist theory, Soviet ethics claims to unite, on a scientific basis, values and facts, ideal and reality, the particular interest of the individual and the general interest of society, even of mankind, as a whole. Moreover, Soviet ethical philosophy claims to be capable of demonstrating the attitude, behavior, and practice which alone will bring about freedom and a humane existence for all. And this practice is individual as well as social, that is to say, it is to unite the individual with a social group on the ground of a common cause by virtue of which the specific concerns of the individual are taken over by the entire group.

Soviet ethics thus claims to weld together ideas and spheres of life that appear as torn asunder in Western ethics. According to the latter, man was to come into his own in a natural and social environment which was compatible with a free and moral existence —at least it did not preclude the attainment of this end. In reality, however, the conditions of life turned out to be rather limiting and hostile, and the environment was experienced, rather, as adverse to the development of an ethical personality. The experience therefore, had to be devaluated and reinterpreted: the "inner man" was separated from his external existence, and the ethical personality was defined in such a way that it included—and even necessitated—renunciation, suffering, and repression. The tension which motivates Western ethics expresses—and at the same time justifies—the experienced contrast between the ever-growing material and intellectual resources and their availability for individual needs, between the demand for self-determination and the limits imposed upon it in reality, between essential equality and the still prevailing inhumanity of man against man, between the ideal of justice and unjust practices. These factual restrictions of the morally sanctioned and professed ideal seem to whittle down the central notions of Western ethics; moreover, they seem to confront human existence with a welter of conflicting loyalties and values (divine versus human, or natural versus positive, law; individual versus commonwealth; private versus public values; family versus social standards). In contrast, Soviet ethics seems to represent the effective solution of these contradictions—an integration of moral with practical values which Western ethics cannot accomplish and does not want to accomplish because it considers the tension between the two spheres as a precondition of moral behavior. The contrast between Western and Soviet ethics may now be illustrated by the different weight given to the values of freedom and security.

The Western idea of freedom is realized through economic and political institutions which are to enable the individual to be the self-responsible architect of his fate. His existence is to be the result of his own activity, that is, his own performance in free competition with other individuals who are about equally equipped. In accordance with this philosophy, the institutionalized safeguards of freedom (the rule of law; civil rights; property guarantees) necessarily leave the individual to his own devices in large areas of his existence. These areas tend to become areas of *insecurity* as the economic process becomes complex and incalculable, beyond the control of the average individual, and dependent on a whole array of supra-individual forces and processes. Freedom in the economic sphere then is canceled by the factual "closing" of whole categories of employment, by the rigidity of prescribed behavior patterns, by the standardization of required work performances, or it involves a risk which the majority of the people cannot afford to take (risk of unemployment, of "falling behind," of becoming an outsider, and so forth). The encroachments on freedom appear as rational and technical processes—nobody's fault and doing, but the by-product (or perhaps even the condition) of the division of labor in late industrial society and, as such, tokens of efficiency and progress. The value itself of freedom seems to become questionable. In reality (though not necessarily in ideology) freedom is being *redefined*. It no longer means being the self-responsible architect of one's life, of one's own potentialities and their realization. Instead, freedom becomes that which the representative political philosophy of ascending individualistic society has always meant it to be, namely, the surrender of the "natural" liberty of the individual to the civil liberty of being able to do what is not prohibited by law or not accessible to law, or, the recognition of legitimate unfreedom.

But this is *security*. The standards of freedom are
shifted from the autonomous individual to the laws
governing the society which governs the individual.
They merge with the laws governing the economy,
the commonwealth, the nation, the alliance of nations.
However, while the individual is supposed to be
made secure within this overwhelming political and
economic cosmos, his "true" freedom is still to derive
from and even to consist of the "inner" being (freedom
of conscience, thought, religion, and so forth). Thus,
while in the factual existence the striving for security
prevails upon the value of freedom and is desired
even at the expense of freedom, freedom and security
come into conflict with each other—a conflict which
can be minimized only by reducing the elements of
independence and autonomy, that is to say, by sacrific-
ing them to the value of security. However, the entire
ideological tradition of Western ethics, with its image
of man as free master and lawgiver, militates against
this trend; and where the latter asserts itself against
all tradition, under the impact of economic necessity,
it only throws in sharper relief the difference between
ideology and reality. The ideology is still strong enough
to block the sanctioning of the surrender of individual
freedom and to counteract total coordination; the
conflict between freedom and security still remains
an avowed condition of existence, and the mastery
of the conflict an ethical task. But the task becomes
ever more unrealistic.

Soviet ethics promises to solve the conflict by supporting the Soviet state in its elimination of the
"negative" aspects of freedom, namely, those areas
in which the individual was still left to his own
devices, although his devices were grossly inadequate
for the great majority of the people. The choice of

education, training, and occupation; the liberty to provide for one's own care and old age; the right to read and write and listen to different and conflicting opinions were reduced or abolished, and Soviet ethics justified this policy. The traditional liberties in these areas succumbed to the regimentation of employment, control of movement, health insurance, censorship, and so forth. The realm of legitimate unfreedom was vastly extended, and the surrender of the "natural" liberty of the individual was openly and methodically enforced in spheres of the human existence which remained sacrosanct in the West. But within the context of Soviet ideology and Soviet objectives, the suppression of traditional liberties assumes a "positive" function which Soviet ethical philosophy interprets as the preparation of true freedom. The traditional liberties can be safely devaluated in Soviet ethics, for, from the Soviet point of view, they are merely ideological or even illusory for the great majority of the population until and unless they are substantiated in economic security, that is, freedom from want.

This independence from want will, according to Marx, only prevail if and when man is no longer enslaved by his labor—in other words, political and intellectual freedom presuppose freedom from the daily struggle for the necessities of life, which in turn presupposes the existence of a classless society. The Marxian conception implies that man ceases to be an economic subject precisely to the degree to which the economy ceases to be his "fate," that is to say, is no longer a determining factor but is itself determined, namely, brought under rational control exercised by the associated individuals. In so far as economic freedom is free competition in the incessant struggle for "earning one's life" (i.e., making a living),

it is, to Marx, the negation of true freedom because it
compels man to spend practically all his time and
energy in procuring the necessities of life—in "alienated labor." And in so far as the notion of the free
individual involves the free economic subject, it is
itself the notion of unfreedom. For the "economy,"
that is, the entire realm of necessity in which the
competitive struggle for existence takes place, cannot
be the realm of individual freedom as long as it is the
realm of alienated labor. To the degree to which this
realm comes under the rational, collective control
of the associated individuals, the "economic subject"
ceases to be essential to the free individual, as do
those liberties which are instruments and supplements
of economic freedom. A large and decisive segment
of what belonged, previously, to the rights of the
private individual then becomes the concern of
society. And if the realm of necessity is brought under
the rational control, not of the associated individuals
but of the state superimposed upon the individuals,
the rights of the individual in this sphere become the
concern of the state.

As the individual changes his social function, so
does the idea of freedom itself. Where the "free
economy" no longer exists, the Western individual is
no longer a reality or even ideology—he is reshaped
and redefined together with his freedom. It is then
incumbent upon society to organize and direct the
production and distribution of the necessities which
are the prerequisites for freedom. And as long as
these necessities are not available to all, and all are
free, the state, as an independent power, is likely
to arrogate to itself this organization and direction,
and with it legislation over the private as well as
public existence of the individual. For no matter

how protected it is, the private remains the "negative" of the public existence, and the individual part of the universal. The state which, as an independent power, controls the realm of necessity, also controls the personal aspirations, objectives, and values of the individual. The systematic reduction of the antagonism between the internal and external, between private and public existence (an antagonism which has become the life element of Western ethics) has been one of the basic functions of Soviet society as well as Soviet ethical philosophy. The inner and private values are externalized, that is to say, man is to be in *all* his manifestations a social and political being.

10

SOVIET ETHICS—
THE EXTERNALIZATION
OF VALUES

The externalization of values is a universal feature of Soviet ethics. It is the concomitant and corollary of rationalization and shares its function and content. Although the abolition of private property is confined to ownership of the means of production, it also affects private property as an existential category.[1]

[1] The ideology according to which private property is essential to the realization of the "free person" is epitomized in Hegel's *Philosophy of Right*, paragraphs 41 ff., especially paragraph 46. However, the extent to which otherwise most fundamentally different thinkers agree on the *essential* connection between the human person and private property is truly remarkable. We may be permitted to recall just a few of the best known statements to this effect:

Thomas Aquinas (*Summa Theologica*, II.ii.qu.66a.1,2): It is not only "lawful" but "necessary" that man should possess property. As regards the use of things, "man has a natural dominion over external things, because by means of his reason and will he can make use of them for his own purpose, as though they were made for him" (trans. Dominican Fathers of the English Province).

John Locke (*Of Civil Government*, Second Treatise, Chap. II, par. 26): Every "man has a 'property' in his own person'. . . . The 'labour' of his body and the 'work' of his hands, we may say, are properly his. Whatsoever, then, he removes out of the state that Nature hath provided and

If private property is no longer regarded as th
instrument through which the individual asserts hin
self, as the expression and embodiment of his se
against other selves, then the whole area of individu
privacy, which has traditionally been permeated wit
the values of private property, becomes externalized-
it becomes the legitimate concern of society. 1
Western ethics, the effects of this externalization a
particularly abhorrent in those two spheres whic
are regarded as the sanctuary and reservoir of th
individual per se, namely, the privacy of though
and conscience, and the privacy of the family. In thes
two spheres perhaps more than in any other, freedor
according to the Western conception, is a functic
of *privacy,* and privacy is linked to property—as th
institution through which the person is legally con
stituted as having a realm of his own. Freedom
thought and conscience requires freedom from inte
ference with matters which belong to the individu;
and not to the state and society. The thoughts an
feelings of the individual and their expression are t
be "his own";[2] he is to utilize and direct them accord
ing to "his own" faculties and conscience; he is n
merely to obey the universal standards but rathe
to "appropriate" them and make them his own (mora
legislation.

Here again, the historical denominator of th

left it in, he has mixed his labour with, and joined to
something that is his own, and thereby makes it his property

Hegel (*Philosophy of Right,* par. 41): "In order that
person be a fully developed and independent organism,
is necessary that he find or make some external sphere for h
freedom. . . . The rationality of property does not lie in i
satisfaction of wants, but in its abrogation of the mere sul
jectivity of personality. It is in property that person primari
exists as reason" (trans. J. M. Sterrett and Carl J. Friedrich

[2] A "natural person" is one "whose words or actions a
considered as his owne." (Hobbes, *Leviathan,* Chap. XVI.

Western conception comes to the fore. The free *privacy* of thought has assumed the dignity of an unconditional right during that period of modern society when the ideas held to be true for the human existence have appeared as *antagonistic* to the truths promulgated or represented by the *public* authorities, especially by the state, by whom those ideas were *not* held valid and self-evident. It is sufficient to recall the fact that "freedom of thought" emerged as a moral and political right in the struggle against feudal and clerical despotism. Even today, where this right has been firmly institutionalized in the Western democracies, its value is activated only in emergency situations in which authoritarian groups and policies encroach upon privacy. Conversely, where there is no real conflict between private thought and public ideology or between private conscience and public morals, freedom of thought and conscience does not seem to be experienced as an essential value on which the individual existence depends—nor does it seem to have an essential content. In the most extreme case, the conflict between private and public values is "resolved" in complete coordination: the individual thinks and feels and values privately what is thought and felt and valued in "public opinion" and expressed in public policies and pronouncements (not necessarily by the government, but by leaders of public opinion, "heroes" and models of aspirations, in general education, and by the predominant forms of entertainment). Such coordination can be established by terror, by the standardizing trends of "mass culture," or by a combination of both. The costs for the individual and for society are incomparably greater if it is accomplished by terror, and the difference may well be that between life and death. However, at the end

of the coordinating process, if and when conformity
has been successfully established, the effect on the
hierarchy of values tends to be the same: individual
freedom of thought and conscience appears to be
losing its independent and unconditional value and
to be submerging in the unification of private and
public existence. In the course of a few generations,
if the effectiveness of the regime is sustained, repres-
siveness may be reduced by spreading over the whole
of society, extending to all parts of the material and
intellectual culture. When privacy and inner freedom
no longer have a definable experiential content, their
abolition no longer has the quality of oppression which
is still attached to it in the Western hierarchy of values.

With the "socialization" of privacy, the locus of
freedom is shifted from the individual as a private
person to the individual as a member of society.
Society as a whole,[3] represented by the Soviet state,
defines not only the value of freedom, but also its
scope, in other words, freedom becomes an instrument
for political objectives.

The instrumentalization of Soviet ethics does not
exclude the consideration of motives and does not
cancel the moral concept of "character." On the contrary, we shall see that motives and character themselves become subject to objective societal evaluation:
the concrete historical situation of Soviet society and
the goals which it is to attain "call for" and define
specific motives and a specific character as *moral.*
The same shift occurs with respect to all other ethical

[3] In Part I of this study, we have emphasized that, in
Soviet Marxism, "society" is made into an independent or at
least separate power over and above its individual members.
In speaking here of "society" as the new denominator for
all ethical values, we refer to this "reification" of society,
which makes it practically coextensive with "the state."

values: they are all referred to a new general denominator, and it is this new common denominator which gives Soviet ethics rational inner consistency and coherence. The individual acts and thinks "morally" in so far as he promotes, in his actions and thoughts, the objectives and values set by society. Ethical value is in this sense "external" to any specific individual action or thought, the latter being instruments for attaining an ethical goal which is that of society. However, while Soviet ethics is essentially instrumentalistic, it is grounded in a new historical position which defines the specific function of communist morality as surpassing instrumentalism.

The function of communist morality was authoritatively defined in Lenin's address to the Third All-Russian Congress of the Communist Youth in 1920,[4] as (1) the negation of the traditional (bourgeois and prebourgeois) morality, that is, the rejection of all ethical values and principles based on transcendental (religious) sanction and/or "idealistic" propositions (Lenin makes no substantive distinction between these two ethics); and (2) the affirmation of a new "communist" morality, which is in its entirety subordinated to the interests of the proletarian class struggle. The principles of this morality are to be derived from the requirements and objectives of this struggle. It must be noted that this exposition of communist morality does not preclude the "taking over" of "bourgeois" ethical values if and when they coincide with the needs of the respective stage of the class struggle. It must also be noted that the avowedly "instrumentalist" character of communist morality (to serve the interests of the proletariat in the class struggle) is,

[4] *Sochineniia* (Works) (3d ed., 30 vols.; Moscow, Institut Lenina, 1928-37), XXX, 403-17.

according to Lenin, directed toward a goal which would surpass the pragmatist level: the purpose of morality is "to raise human society to a higher stage and to liberate it from exploitation."

As to the specific content of communist morality: "For the communist, the entire morality consists in the firm solidarity and discipline [of the class struggle] and in the conscious struggle of the masses against the exploiters." [5] Lenin's definition points up the absence of all specifically ethical values apart from and outside the class struggle (a necessary result of the historical position of communist morality), and, at the same time, indicates the direction in which these values will subsequently be concretized. "Solidarity and discipline" focus communist ethics on the rigid work morale of the Stalinist period, while the emphasis on the *conscious* struggle (reiterated throughout Lenin's address) reveals the strongly "intellectualist" character of Soviet ethics—learning, training, the systematic and methodical appropriation of the technical and cultural knowledge accumulated in civilization is made one of the foremost prerequisites for the building of communism. In this respect, too, Soviet ethical philosophy claims to be the heir of the Western rationalist tradition: the attainment of freedom, in other words, the realization of man, is to be based on knowledge and reason.

Lenin's primitive and brutal definition of communist morality presupposes a complex historical dialectic which is to raise these ethics from the realm of relative to that of absolute validity. The "higher stage of human society" (the stage of total and universal liberation) would cancel the specific character of

[5] *Ibid.,* XXX, 413.

communist morality and make the instrument an end in itself.

The instrumentalistic character of Soviet ethics has been made the main target of Western criticism, and this criticism has been focused on the principle that "the end justifies the means"—a principle which is considered as unethical in itself. However, Soviet ethics aims beyond instrumentalism, and the critique in terms of the means-end relation misses the target. The suprapragmatic tendencies of Soviet ethics derive from the specific features of Soviet instrumentalism.

The society which provides the general denominator for Soviet ethics is, according to Soviet philosophy, defined by two essential characteristics (they were more fully discussed in Part I): (1) It is supposed to be organized in such a way that it has established the *preconditions* for the free development and fulfillment of all humane faculties for all its members (by the abolition of private control over the means of production and, thereby, of exploitation and class justice). (2) Owing to the particular circumstances of "backwardness" and "capitalist environment," these conditions for freedom have not yet been fully utilized for the immediate benefit of the individuals. Repression, scarcity, and unproductive use of the productive forces (production of armaments) still prevail (marks of the lower stage of socialism as distinguished from the higher stage of communism). The conditions of freedom are thus still preconditions; their realization depends on the continued exertion of the still unfree individuals.

The interrelation of these two conceptions of society gives Soviet instrumentalism its specific dynamic. The first (affirmative) conception furnishes a set of

objective ethical standards, that is to say, those pertaining to a fully developed classless society ("communism"). These standards recapture the traditional
ideal of Western civilization—freedom, justice, and
the all-round development of the individual—condensed in the formula: "From each according to his
abilities; to each according to his needs." The formula
reestablishes the individual as the ultimate point of
reference for ethical norms: what furthers the free
development of the individual is good. The extreme
relativism inherent in this norm is supposedly freed
from harmful connotations by the socialist institutions: the general will is to coincide with the will of
all individuals; the inequality of needs and faculties
becomes an absolute value if and when it no longer
involves the development of one individual at the
expense of others. The prospective end result of
socialist morality thus bestows upon Soviet ethics the
dignity of universally valid and objective norms, culminating in the principle of solidarity and cooperation.
Instrumentalism terminates in ethical absolutism; par-
tisanship and class morality are proclaimed as mere
vehicles (although the *only* historical vehicles) for
the realization of *humanitas*. These standards of the
future are then related to the actual situation of Soviet
society, but they retain their "transcendental" connotation, that is, the image of a future which will
compensate the individuals for their present sufferings
and frustrations. Soviet ethics here contains a "safety
valve": the image of the future seems to perform a
function corresponding to that of the transcendental
elements of Western ethics—in this image we seem
to have a real Soviet substitute for religion. However,
there is an essential difference from which Soviet
ethics derives much of its appeal. The transcendental

goal in Soviet ethics is a historical one, and the road to its attainment a historical process—the result of a concrete social and political development. Final human fulfillment and gratification are not oriented on the "inner self" or the hereafter, but on the "next stage" of the actual development of society. And the truth of this conception is to be, not a matter of faith, but a matter of scientific analysis and reason—of necessity.[6]

Unquestionably, this official argument for Soviet ethics serves well to justify a repressive regime which may use it only as an ideological veil for the perpetuation of the present state. However, what holds true for the Soviet use of Marxism in general[7] may also be applied to its ethical philosophy: once it has become an essential part of the psychical and behavioral structure of the individuals, once it has become a factor of social cohesion and integration, it assumes a momentum of its own and moves under its own weight. Only as such a factor, not as an objective of the Soviet leadership, is Soviet ethics considered in the context of this study. The claim that it is founded on objective historical necessity gives Soviet ethics an extreme rigidity but also a greatly increased

---

[6] To be sure, the ideology of *progress*, which rationalizes the present deprivation, suffering, and repression as preconditions of their eventual disappearance, is also inherent in the Western bourgeois tradition—as a matter of fact, it is even "taken over" from this tradition. However, two facts constitute the decisive difference: (1) The religion of technical-scientific progress has never been sanctioned as the avowed goal and expression of humanist development. The schools of thought which came closest to this philosophy (for example, that of Saint-Simon) were always considered as suspect and "heretic." (2) By the same token, Western ethics refused to accept the straight correspondence between (technical) progress and ethics. Here too, the tension (and even conflict) between these two remained itself a mainspring of morality.

[7] See Part I of this study.

scope and intensity. Precisely because it is relative to
an absolute end, in this sense "outside" any specific
individual action and position, Soviet ethics regards as
immoral all actions and positions which run counter
to or retard the alleged historical necessity. Many
areas of human existence, which, in the Western tradition, are morally "neutral," thus become subject to
moral evaluation, for example, the area of scientific
and artistic pursuits. A scientific theory, though it
may be scientifically corroborated, may be condemned
if it is deemed to be detrimental to communist
morality. The epistemological notion of truth (theoretical reason) and the moral notion of good (practical
reason) tend to converge—just as, in the sphere of
art and literature, aesthetic truth tends to converge
with epistemological truth.[8] They converge in the
medium of politics which coordinates the traditionally
separated spheres of human existence as well as the
values reflecting this separation. Moreover, the new
historical basis of Soviet ethics also necessitates the
application of moral judgments to "neutral" areas in
the private sphere—again through the medium of
politics. A love relationship with a "class enemy" is
morally condemnable because it is politically "wrong"
—particularly if it is a true love relationship. For
then it engages the entire existence of the individual
and not only the "private" part of his existence, and
thus it affects his relationship to others, to work, and
to the state. Consequently, in so far as ethical standards apply to it at all, the same standards as the
political ones apply—there is no dual morality. Soviet
ethics is political instrumentalism—but so that the

[8] See pp. 117 f. above.

political sphere is not one among others, but rather that it is *the* sphere of human realization.

Politicalization of ethics stands at the beginning and at the end of Western philosophy. In both, Plato and Hegel, the autonomy of ethics succumbs to (or rather is transformed into) the autonomy of the *res publica,* the state. And in both, not relativistic pragmatism but absolutism is the result. If the "idea of the good" demands the Polis for its realization or approximation, then the good is attainable only in the *bios politicos;* and the Polis embodies the absolute ethical standards. It embodies them—which means that it is not the ultimate good itself. However, for the realization of human existence, the moral good presupposes the political good; and the latter is defined in terms of the resources, institutions, and relationships which allow the best possible realization of man (of his essence as a "rational being"). According to this conception, the ethical conflict is, not between the (moral) individual and the (amoral) Polis, not between two antagonistic moralities, but between moral and immoral behavior *in* the Polis. Socrates represents, not the right of the individual against that of the Polis, but the right against the wrong Polis. It is not private freedom of thought and conscience that is at stake, but political thought and conscience, that is, the Polis, which is accepted by both Socrates and his judges. Ethical and political philosophy, ethics and politics, have a common epistemological basis: truth in ethics and politics derives from knowledge of the objectively true order in nature and society. Ethical truth is thus political truth, and political truth is *absolute* truth. Essentially the same conception survives in Marxian theory, especially in the treatment of ideology. We have noted that Soviet statements on intellectual culture recall, even in their formulation Plato's *Republic* and *Laws*.[9]

In order to understand the full implications of the Soviet conception, it is advisable to identify its deep roots in the very civilization which it challenges. The usage of the word "totalitarianism" as a catchall for the Platonic, Hegelian, Fascist, and Marxian philosophies readily serves to cover up the historical link between totalitarianism and its opposite, and the historical reasons which caused classical humanism to turn into its negation.

As long as the humanistic values, and particularly freedom, are not translated into reality, their very content remains subject to the conditions under which they can be translated into reality. This translation is a political one because it involves society as a whole and not only the private individual. The realization of freedom is thus an objective process in a twofold sense: (1) it implies the transformation of an established society, and (2) this transformation depends on the respective historical conditions. On both grounds, the realization of freedom presupposes thought and action (theory and practice) in accordance with the historical truth, that is, with objective reason. Then this theory and practice, and not the preservation of isolated individual freedom, appears as the primary ethical task and ethical value. The verification of the "right" theory and practice, the validation of objective reason, may be sought in idealistic ontology or in dialectical materialism—the two systems are on opposite philosophical poles, but they both imply the *transitional absorption of freedom*

[9] See p. 117 above.

into historical and political necessity, that is, into objective reason.

The common ground is laid in Hegel's philosophy. We have pointed out that the Soviet Marxist notion of freedom restates Engels's paraphrase of Hegel's conception: freedom is "recognition of necessity" and action in accordance with recognized necessity.[1] It is more than questionable whether this paraphrase gives the real meaning of Hegel's notion; still, it is true that, in Hegel's system, the private sphere of freedom is dissolved into the public sphere of State and Law, and subjective rights are dissolved into objective truths. It has often been remarked that there is no special discipline of "ethics" in the otherwise all-embracing Hegelian system. The power which makes for this "disappearance" of independent ethical philosophy and for the dissolution of private ethical values is *History.*

This is the point where the politicalization of ethics, which grew out of the Western tradition, consolidated into a new system of thought claiming to be the heir as well as the adversary, the fulfillment as well as the negation, of this tradition. The progress of Western civilization itself placed on the agenda the translation of internal values into external conditions, of subjective ideas into objective reality, and of ethics into politics. If Hegel interpreted Reason in terms of history, he anticipated, in an idealistic formulation, the Marxian transition from theory to practice. The historical process has created the preconditions, both material and intellectual, for the realization of Reason (Hegel) in the organization of society (Marx), for the convergence of freedom and necessity. However,

[1] See p. 136 above.

freedom which converges with (or is even absorbed by) necessity is not the final form of freedom. At this ultimate point, Hegel and Marx again agree. The realm of true freedom is beyond the realm of necessity. Freedom as well as necessity are redefined. For Hegel, ultimate freedom resides in the realm of the Absolute Spirit. For Marx, the realm of necessity is to be mastered by a society whose reproduction has been subjected to the control of the individuals, and freedom is the free play of individual faculties outside the realm of necessary labor. Freedom is "confined" to free time—but free time is, quantitatively and qualitatively, the very content of life. Moreover, according to Marx, the historical process, governed by objective laws, generates socialism as the rational organization of the conditions for freedom through the political activity of the proletariat. Historical necessity thus turns ethics into politics, and insight into historical necessity anchors politics on "scientific" grounds and gives politics an objective character. On such grounds, Soviet ethical philosophy presents itself as the very opposite of "bourgeois" opportunism, pragmatism, and irrationalism—as the protagonist of Reason against the destroyers of Reason. The attack on bourgeois ethical philosophy is waged on behalf of the "betrayed" rationalistic tradition.

The struggle against bourgeois ethics becomes the more vital for Soviet social philosophy the more the two seem to have certain features in common. The progressive, critical trends in bourgeois philosophy become the chief target of the attack, and the chief indictment leveled against them is that of the defamation of Reason. Nietzsche and Freud, Schopenhauer and Dewey, pragmatism, existentialism, and logical positivism are branded as irrationalistic, anti-intellectualistic—and by this token "reactionary," "immoral," and "imperialistic." According to Soviet interpretation, they are necessarily so—in their objective historical function—no matter what the personal intentions and convictions of the respective philosophers may have been. For any compromise with the historically surpassed values of bourgeois society, any attempt to deny the objective validity of the historically defined direction of progress and of man's capacity to grasp it, appears to this conception as justification of an obsolescent social system.

It is not necessary here to follow the course of this criticism: we shall merely attempt to show the method which it applies. (It is largely the same that prevails in the Marxist critique of capitalism and that gives this critique its rational appeal.) One of the main elements of this method is to assume the validity of the adversary's ideas and objectives, to accept them, as it were, and then to show that they are unrealizable within the theoretical and societal framework in which the adversary operates. Consequently, they are being betrayed, vitiated, or made illusory by bourgeois philosophy and its society. In the case of ethical philosophy, the two chief targets of Soviet criticism are: (*a*) the effort of contemporary Western ethics to come to grips with the concrete existential situation of the individual and to derive from this situation the conceptual and practical tools for progress in freedom and reason; and (*b*) the attempt to give ethics a scientific (logical or experimental) basis. These objectives, according to the Soviet critique, not only cannot be attained by bourgeois ethical theorists, but, in the effort to attain them they are being turned into their opposite. In so far as progressive bourgeois ethics works with the institutions and ideologies of capitalist society, it sustains the very forces which prevent progress. Thus denying the higher historical stage of reason and freedom which implies the elimination of capitalism, this philosophy is irrational and abstract where it claims to be rational and concrete: it retains an obsolete definition of reason, and it disregards (abstracts from) the concrete historical conditions of freedom. By virtue of this position, progressive bourgeois ethics is regressive even where it is critical of the established society. Moreover, Soviet theory rejects Western philosophy the more violently the more the latter is critical, because, in the Soviet view, the bourgeois critique of present-day society, while pointing up its repressive features, at the same time diverts the struggle against the causes of repression. The scientific devices and paraphernalia of this philosophy are alleged to be spurious and to fulfill the function of obscuring and withdrawing attention from the real issues, that is, the stagnation and the destructiveness of the capitalist system. We shall illustrate this interpretation by the Soviet treatment of Dewey's pragmatism.

There seems to be a close affinity between Marx's and Dewey's reorientation of theory on practice. However, the Soviet critique emphasizes that Marxism and pragmatism are not only essentially different but opposed to each other. As formulated by Shariia, according to the Marxist thesis, "not that which is useful is true, but that which is true is useful." [2] The formulation refers to Lenin's *Materialism and Empiriocriticism*. There, Lenin had stated that to the Marxist, practice is the criterion of truth only in so far as it is

---

[2] P. Shariia, *O nekotorykh voprosakh kommunisticheskoi morali* (On Several Problems of Communist Morality) (Moscow, Gospolitizdat, 1951), p. 220.

itself derived from true knowledge and cognition,[3] and in so far as it is the practice of that social group which is alone capable of recognizing and fulfilling the truth, namely, the class-conscious proletariat. The Marxian unity of theory and practice presupposes the existence of an objective, even "absolute" truth, to be demonstrated by dialectical materialism (for example, the truth about the potentialities and prospects of a society, and thus the truth about the potentialities and prospects of freedom and "growth"). The content of this truth is historical, and so is its accessibility and its realization, but these relative elements are the characteristics of the objective reality and of the objective truth about this reality. According to Lenin, dialectics "includes" relativism, but does not "reduce itself" to relativism; relative are only the historical conditions for the "approach" to and for the realization of the objective truth.[4] Applied to morality, this position permits not only the rejection of certain supposedly unconditional moral principles as ideological distortions of the objective truth, but also the acceptance of certain "elementary principles" of human morality *independent of class content*.[5] Since the rejection of the moral libertinism of the early twenties, Soviet ethical philosophy places increasing emphasis on the fact that the Marxian thesis, according to which the societal existence of man determines his consciousness, does not vitiate the validity of general ethical norms. For no matter how different the historical modes of societal existence are, certain basic relationships and behavior patterns are common to all

[3] *Sochineniia* (Works), XIII, 112-17.
[4] *Ibid.*, XIII, 107-12.
[5] Shariia, *O nekotorykh voprosakh kommunisticheskoi morali,* Chap. VIII. See also pp. 63 f.

forms of civilized society, and they are expressed in certain general "rules of ethical conduct" which are valid for all men, regardless of class. The Soviet Marxist insistence on the general validity of ethical principles closely parallels the Soviet Marxist position on language and logic; it was this same argument that was applied in the defense of formal logic against the attempts to dissolve the latter into dialectical logic,[6] and also against the class doctrine of language.

These ideological trends express the development by virtue of which the Soviet state loses its unique revolutionary position and partakes of the organizational and behavioral pattern characteristic of contemporary industrial civilization. At this stage, long-range rationalization, efficiency, and calculability become primary economic and political requirements. The stress on objective truths in ethics belongs to the recent efforts to bring the ideology in line with the new stage of Soviet society. But the latter also requires insistence on the claim that the Soviet society alone is on the right historical road toward the realization of these truths. The objective principles of Soviet ethics are thus of a twofold character: they claim (1) to refer to the moral principles valid for any form of civilized society, and (2) to pertain to the socialist society which alone can realize genuine freedom and justice. From the first position Soviet moral philosophy assails all bourgeois ethics labeled prefascist or fascist which deny universal moral principles in favor of such amoral forces as Life, Will to Power, Eros, and so forth. The second position is the center of the attack against Dewey.

The assault against "bourgeois irrationalism" is particularly illuminating because it reveals the traits common to the Soviet and Western rationality, namely, the

[6] In the logic discussion of 1950-51; see Part I of this study, pp. 132 f. above.

prevalence of technological elements over humanistic ones. Schopenhauer and Nietzsche, the various schools of "vitalism" (*Lebensphilosophie*), existentialism, and depth psychology differ and even conflict in most essential aspects; however, they are akin in that they explode the technological rationality of modern civilization. They do so by pointing up the psychical and biological forces beneath this rationality and the unredeemable sacrifices which it exacts from man. The result is a transvaluation of values which shatters the ideology of progress—not by romanticist and sentimental regression, but by breaking into tabooed dimensions of bourgeois society itself. This transvaluation acts upon precisely those values which Soviet society must protect at all cost: the ethical value of competitive performance, socially necessary labor, self-perpetuating work discipline, postponed and repressed happiness. Thus, Soviet Marxism, in its fight against "bourgeois values," cannot recognize and accept the most destructive critique of these values in the "bourgeois camp" itself; instead, it has to deny these critics by isolating and ridiculing the (obviously) regressive aspects of their philosophy.

The attack against Dewey takes a different direction. Since his pragmatism does not recognize any objective evaluation which condemns bourgeois society as historically obsolescent, his effort to overcome the ideological limits of bourgeois ethics must necessarily end in conformistic relativism. Dewey opposes to the unscientific absolutism of the ethical idealists the infinite plurality of existential situations, experiences, and aspirations, each with its own potentialities of "growth" and therefore with its own values. However, such a plurality, according to Soviet criticism, is not per se a ground for positive ethical evaluation. It can provide such a ground only where the society which

integrates the plurality of situations and goals affords
the real possibility of free "growth." Now Marxism
maintains that precisely such a possibility cannot exist
in the "declining" bourgeois society—except in marginal cases and at the expense of others. The refusal
to transcend beyond this society into its "objective"
historical future therefore vitiates Dewey's efforts to
overcome a conformistic ethical relativism. To be sure,
Dewey's pragmatism does not exclude social change
and reform: they are to be promoted by education for
true and full knowledge, and this knowledge in turn
is to guide gradual reform. However, this program is
self-contradictory, according to the Soviet critics;
society cannot grant the educational facilities and
rights to a knowledge which would make for the
destruction of this society. This situation compels
Dewey's philosophy to accept implicitly (and perhaps
even against the intentions of Dewey himself) the
standards and goals prevalent in the established society. Moreover, it also condemns Dewey's attempt to
found ethics on a scientific basis. The frame of reference within which Dewey's propositions are to be
verified is the institutional and ideological system of
bourgeois society, which is itself in need of "verification." Short of such transcending verification (which
would show that the framework is faulty), Dewey's
"science of conduct" amounts simply to a description
(and even justification) of socially prevalent conduct.
The refusal to extend the scientific method into the
historical future, which is accessible to science through
the analysis of the fundamental trends in the present
society, confines pragmatism to a mere description of
what is.[7]

[7] Shariia, *O nekotorykh voprosakh kommunisticheskoi morali*
(On Several Problems of Communist Morality), pp. 24, 85 f.,
223.

11

THE PRINCIPLES OF
COMMUNIST MORALITY

According to the Soviet interpretation of its ethical position, we should expect two levels of moral philosophy: one defining the "elementary principles of human morality independent of class content," and another showing the expression of these principles, and their specific realization in "communist morality." However, we are confronted with the problem that there seems to be no systematic exposition of the former which could adequately provide representative material for analysis. The lack of any systematic derivation of the "elementary principles of human morality" is, of course, inherent in the politicalization of ethics: the more the moral values become political values and the more moral behavior becomes right political behavior, the less room there is for *independent* ethical principles, or rather for the derivation of their objective validity. Still, Soviet ethics claims objective validity in so far as the specific goals of Soviet society are to coincide with the universal interest of mankind, namely, the interest in the realization of freedom for all. But this is also the claim of "bourgeois ethics." *Formally,* the "elementary principles of human moral-

ity" assumed by Soviet moral philosophy will thus
coincide with those assumed by its antagonist. By the
same token, the universally valid principles tend to
merge with the specific principles of communist morality. Within the context of Soviet ethics, the former
receive their real significance from the latter, which
in turn are defined in accord with the development of
Soviet society. Therefore, presently, we shall discuss
these principles in terms of their social and political
function. And from the first step on, we are confronted
with the fact that, to a striking degree, the specific
principles of communist morality as well as the universal "principles of human morality" resemble those
of bourgeois ethics. Just as the Soviet constitution, in
the proclamation of the "Fundamental Rights and
Duties of Citizens" seems to copy the "bourgeois-
democratic" ideology and practice, so do the Soviet
statements of ethical principles. It is needless to emphasize the difference between ideology and reality—
the fact of imitation or assimilation remains. The
world-historical coexistence of the two competing systems, which defines their political dynamic, also defines
the social *function* of their ethics.

In going through the enumerations of the highest
moral values given in Soviet ethical philosophy, it is
difficult to find a single moral idea or syndrome of
moral ideas that is not common to Western ethics.
Care, responsibility, love, patriotism, diligence, hon-
esty, industriousness, the injunctions against trans-
gressing the happiness of one's fellow men, consideration for the common interest—there is nothing in this
catalogue of values that could not be included in the
ethics of the Western tradition. The similarity continues to prevail if we look at the specific principles of

communist morality.[1] The hierarchy of values stated by Lenin in 1920 is almost literally repeated; the moral norms added to it are hardly more than a reformulation with respect to the situation of a fully and firmly established Soviet state. Soviet patriotism; national pride in the Soviet state; international, national, and individual solidarity; respect for socialist property; love for socialist labor; love, loyalty, and responsibility for the socialist family and for the Party—in order to be able to evaluate the actual function of these commonplace notions, we have to place them in the concrete context in which they are illustrated in Soviet ethics. This context is provided by the discussion of work relations, marriage and family matters, leisure activities, and education, and by their presentation in literature and in the entertainment industry. The moral values converge on the subordination of pleasure to duty—the duty to put everything one has into service for the State, the Party, and society. Translated into private morality, this means strict monogamic relations, directed toward the production and raising of children; discipline and competitive performance in the established division of functions; and leisure activities as relaxation from work and re-creation of energy for work rather than as an end in itself. It is in every respect a *competitive work morality,* proclaimed with a rigidity surpassing that of bourgeois morality— softened or hardened according to the specific interests of the Soviet state (for example, softened as in the treatment of illegitimate children, or if rigidity comes into conflict with the requirements of political loyalty,

---

[1] See also N. I. Boldyrev, *V. I. Lenin i I. V. Stalin o vospitanii kommunisticheskoi morali* (V. I. Lenin and J. V. Stalin on the Training of a Communist Morality) (Moscow, *Pravda,* 1951).

work efficiency, party discipline, and so forth; hardened as in the punishment for theft or "sabotage" of state property).

One of the most representative exhortations designed to "strengthen communist morale" [2] is entirely centered on work morale. The "highest principles" governing this morale are said to be Soviet patriotism and love for the motherland, which are joined with "proletarian internationalism." They serve as justification for the complete endorsement of work as the very content of the individual's whole life. Not only is work itself honor and glory, and "socialist competition" an unconditional duty, *all* work, under socialism, has a creative character, and any degradation of manual labor impairs communist education. In Soviet society, "love for one's work" is per se one of the highest principles of communist morality, and work per se is declared to be one of the most important factors in the building of moral qualities. In view of the moral value of work in a socialist society, the differences between intellectual and manual labor, between elevated and lowly work, become irrelevant.

This moral equalization of the various modes and spheres of work is of the greatest significance for defining the actual function of Soviet ethics. Marxian theory made an essential distinction between work as the realization of human potentialities and work as "alienated labor"; the entire sphere of material production, of mechanized and standardized performances, is considered as one of alienation. By virtue of this distinction, the realization of freedom is attributed to a social organization of labor fundamentally differ-

[2] "Neustanno vospityvat' sovetskikh liudei v dukhe kommunisticheskoi morali" (Unceasingly Educate Soviet People in the Spirit of Communist Morality), *Kommunist* (Communst), 1954, No. 13 (September), pp. 3-12.

ent from the prevailing one, to a society where work as the free play of human faculties has become a "necessity," a "vital need" for society, while work for procuring the necessities of life no longer constitutes the working day and the occupation of the individual. It is in the last analysis the abolition of alienation which, for Marx, defines and justifies socialism as the "higher stage" of civilization. And socialism in turn defines a new human existence: its content and value are to be determined by free time rather than labor time, that is to say, man comes into his own only outside and "beyond" the entire realm of material production for the mere necessities of life. Socialization of production is to reduce the time and energy spent in this realm to a minimum, and to maximize time and energy for the development and satisfaction of individual needs in the realm of freedom.

In contrast with this conception, Soviet work morale does not recognize any difference in the value of alienated and nonalienated labor: the individual is supposed to invest all his energy and all his aspirations in whatever function he finds himself or is put by the authorities. It is this obliteration of the decisive difference between alienated and nonalienated labor which enables Soviet Marxism to proclaim for the Soviet system the full development of the all-round individual as against the mutilated individual of Western society.[3] But application of Marx's and Engels's notion of a communist society to the Soviet-socialist construction of communism only points up the contrast between the Marxian and the Soviet notion: in the latter, the full development of the individual is that of

[3] Igor' Semenovich Kon, *Razvitie lichnosti pri sotsializme* (The Development of Personality under Socialism) (Leningrad, Vsesoiuznoe obshchestvo po rasprostraneniiu politicheskikh i nauchnykh znanii, 1954), pp. 3 ff.

the all-round laborer, investing his individuality in his labor. It is claimed that the "very character of labor under socialism has changed"; consequently, "every person" is "required to work according to his capabilities for the good of the people and for himself." There is nothing socialist or communist in this formula—as long as the work according to his capabilities is still work within "the realm of necessity," that is, as long as it is not yet the free play of human faculties.

The considerable relaxation which has recently been proclaimed and implemented has not eliminated the merging of technical and moral standards, of labor productivity and ethics, efficiency and happiness. Under the old slogan of the fight against the remnants of capitalist influence in the mentality of the people, a systematic struggle is still being fought against all libertarian tendencies which might endanger the objectives of the regime.

Soviet Marxism links the survival of capitalist elements to the continuation of the "capitalist environment." The Western powers are accused of trying to reactivate those remnants of the past which still have a foothold inside the Soviet state. But the struggle against capitalist ideologies and attitudes has significance primarily for domestic policy: it is to counteract the danger of relaxation involved in growing productivity. Moreover, and perhaps even more important, it is to improve and augment a well-trained, skilled, and disciplined labor force. The fight against the heritage of the past thus greatly resembles early capitalism's own fight against precapitalist values and attitudes.[4]

[4] M. M. Rozental, *Marksistskii dialekticheskii metod* (Marxist Dialectical Method) (Moscow, Gospolitizdat, 1951), p. 303.

The ideological reeducation is still centered on the "socialist" attitude toward work, instead of the negative attitude said to be characteristic of and appropriate to the worker in an exploitative society. The demand for positive identification of the worker with his work, the pressure for relentless "socialist emulation," continues in all fields. According to Soviet statements, the pressure seems to be successful:

In the development of the new attitude toward work, socialist competition played a major role. From the first "Communist Saturdays" (unpaid work) born in the years of civil war, to the storm brigades of the period of the country's large-scale industrialization, to the mass movements of pioneers in industrial innovation—such are the main stages in the development of socialist competition. If participants in Communist Saturdays were only advanced groups of workers, socialist competition and the storm-brigade movement in the late 1920s and early 1930s already encompassed the greater part of the workers who participate in socialist competition, and the number of innovation pioneers among them increases incessantly.[5]

Stakhanovism is presented as creating the preconditions for the "all-round development of the personality." [6] Just as the withering away of the state is to be

[5] G. Glezerman, "Tvorcheskaia rol' narodnykh mass v razvitii sotsialisticheskogo obshchestva" (The Creative Role of the National Masses in the Development of Socialist Society), *Kommunist* (Communist), 1955, No. 3 (February), p. 48. In an article on "Recent Trends in Soviet Labor Policy" (*Monthly Labor Review*, July, 1956) Jerzy G. Glicksman draws attention to the fact that "Stakhanovism underwent modifications." As a result of the rapid technological progress after the Second World War, emphasis shifted from "physical effort, individual pacemaking, and record breaking to the search for new working processes leading to technical progress and that mastering and widespread application of these processes" (p. 6). However important this modification may be, it does not change the function of Stakhanovism as streamlining of alienated labor.

[6] Ts. A. Stepanian, "Usloviia i puti perekhoda ot sotsializma k kommunizmu" (The Conditions and the Paths of the Tran-

preceded by the strengthening of the state, so the abolition of toil is to be preceded by the intensification of toil.

By definition, there is no alienated labor in Soviet society because production is nationalized. But nationalization does not preclude alienation. The latter prevails as long as (socially necessary) labor time is the measure of social wealth.

For true wealth is the developed productivity of all individuals. Then, no longer labor time but free time (disposable time) is the measure of wealth. Using labor time as the measure of wealth places wealth itself on the foundation of poverty . . . and makes the entire time of the individual into labor time, thereby degrading him to a mere laborer, subsuming him under his labor. The most highly developed machinery therefore forces the laborer now to work longer than the savage did, or longer than he himself did with the most primitive, the simplest tools.[7]

The denial of alienation in Soviet ethics may at first appear as a mere subtlety of abstract theorizing; however, upon closer analysis, it reveals the concrete substance of Soviet ethical philosophy. In canceling the notion of alienation as applicable to Soviet society, Soviet ethics removes the moral ground from under the protest against a repressive social organization of labor and adjusts the moral structure and the character of the individual to this organization. Laboring in the service of the Soviet state is per se ethical—the true vocation of Soviet man. The individual needs and aspirations are disciplined; renumeration and toil is the road to salvation. The theory and practice which were to lead to a new life in freedom are turned into

sition from Socialism to Communism), in *O sovetskom sotsialisticheskom obshchestve* (On Soviet Socialist Society), ed. by F. Konstantinov (Moscow, Gospolitizdat, 1948), p. 502.
[7] Marx, *Grundrisse der Kritik der Politischen Oekonomie* (Berlin, Dietz, 1953), p. 596.

instruments of training men for a more productive, more intense, and more rational mode of labor. What the Calvinist work morale achieved though strengthening irrational anxiety about forever-hidden divine decisions, is here accomplished through more rational means: a more satisfying human existence is to be the reward for the growing productivity of labor. And in both cases, far more telling economic and physical force guarantee their effectiveness. The resemblance is more than incidental: the two ethics meet on the common ground of historical "contemporaneousness"— they reflect the need for the incorporation of large masses of "backward" people into a new social system, the need for the creation of a well-trained, disciplined labor force, capable of vesting the perpetual routine of the working day with ethical sanction, producing ever more rationally ever increasing amounts of goods, while the rational use of these goods for the individual needs is ever more delayed by the "circumstances." In this sense, Soviet ethics testifies to the *similarity* between Soviet society and capitalist society. The basis for the similarity was established in the Stalinist period.

In the development of Soviet society, the Stalinist period is that of industrialization, or rather "industrial civilization" in the sense outlined by Lenin in his last writings,[8] with the far-reaching principal objective of "catching up" with and surpassing the level of productivity prevailing in the advanced Western countries. Given the starting point for industrialization in the backward state of Bolshevik Russia, this period would correspond to the early stages of capitalist industrialization, after the "primary accumulation" had been completed.

[8] See pp. 33 f. in Part I of this study.

However, the advantageous position of the "late-comer," nationalization of the means of production, central planning, and totalitarian control, makes it possible for the Soviet state to telescope several stages of industrialization, to utilize the most rationalized technology and machinery, advanced science, and the most intensive working methods without being seriously hampered by conflicting private interests. Soviet ethical philosophy formulates the basic values of primary industrialization, but it also expresses, simultaneously, the different (and even conflicting) requirements of the later stages. Soviet ethics must combine the need for "primary" disciplining of the laboring classes with the need for individual initiative and responsibility—the standardized compliance of the human tool with the intelligent imagination of the engineer. It must foster a morale conducive to a long working day as well as to a high productivity of labor, to quantitative as well as qualitative performance. The conditions of backwardness which defined Soviet industrialization have met with those of advanced technology (eighteenth-century with twentieth-century industrialism)—in the political institutions as well as in the ethics of Soviet society. Administrative absolutism faces the effective constitutionalism of the democratic West, a privileged authoritarian bureaucracy must be refined and renewed and kept open to ascent from below. This is required not only by the need to increase the scope and efficiency of the productive apparatus, but also by the obvious competition with the capabilities and realities of the Western world. Increasing cultural and material compensations for the underlying population are indispensable—not only for political reasons, but also on economic grounds; they belong to the "development of the productive forces" which constitutes the backbone of long-range Soviet policy.[9]

Soviet ethics tries to integrate this diversity of economic and political needs and to translate it into a coherent system of moral values. Thus one finds side by side the exhortation to individual initiative and spontaneity and to authoritarian discipline, to Stachanovist competition and to socialist equality; the glorification of work and the glorification of leisure, of toil and of freedom, of totalitarian and of democratic values. Soviet social philosophy reflects throughout the objective historical contradiction inherent in Soviet society—a contradiction generated by the fact that the principles of socialist economy were made into an instrument of domination, to be applied to a backward country confronted with a far more advanced capitalist world. The need for "catching up" with capitalism called for enforced and accelerated industrialization as the only available road to socialism. While the humanist values attached to the *end* of the road became ritualized into ideology, the values attached to the *means,* i.e., the values of total industrialization, became the really governing values. (In Part I of this study,[1] we have speculated on the possibility that in some not too unforeseeable future the present communist parties outside the Soviet orbit—and perhaps even within it—may become heirs to the traditional Social Democratic parties. Here we seem to hit upon a striking parallel in the ideological field. The end recedes, the means becomes everything; and the sum total of means is "the movement" itself. It absorbs and adorns itself with the values of the goal, whose realization "the movement" itself delays. Was not this the

[9] See pp. 97 f., 171 f. above.
[1] See pp. 57 f.

implicit and explicit philosophy of German Socia
Democracy since Eduard Bernstein?) Socialist moral
ity thus succumbs to industrial morality, while th
various historical stages of the latter are condensed
into one comprehensive unit, combining elements from
the ethics of Calvinism and Puritanism, enlightened
absolutism and liberalism, nationalism, chauvinism
and internationalism, capitalist and socialist values
This is the strange syndrome presented by Sovie
ethics.

Within this syndrome, the repressive elements are
predominant. Many of the rules of conduct in school
and home, at work and leisure, in private and in public
resemble so much their traditional Western counter
parts at earlier stages that they have the sound of
secular sermons documenting the "spirit of Protestant
capitalist ethics." They are not too far from Puritan
exhortations to good business. The praise of the mono
gamic family and of the joy and duty of conjugal love
recalls classical "petty-bourgeois ideology," while the
dissolution of the sphere of privacy reflects twentieth
century reality. The struggle against prostitution, adul
tery, and divorce evokes the same ethical norms as in
the West, while the requirements of the birth rate and
the sustained investment of energy in competitive
work performances are praised as manifestations of
Eros. To be sure, the public exhortations to combine
erotic relations with meritorious occupational perform
ance should not be taken too seriously: there is evi
dence of official and semi-official ridicule and protest
and of widespread private transgression. What is
decisive is the general trend, and the extent to which
the individual's own evaluation of his personal rela
tionships agrees with the politically desired evaluation

Relaxation recently has been widespread, but with

ut changing the underlying morality. The trend seems
o be toward normalization rather than abolition of
epression. In line with tendencies prevalent in late
adustrial civilization, repression is to be "spontane-
usly" reproduced by the repressed individuals; this
llows a relaxation of external, compulsory repression.
'he popular and official protests against the subordina-
on of love to work morale may provide an illustra-
on. They are rigidly antilibertarian; they emphasize
tat love, responsibility, family morale, and even hap-
iness are duties to the state:

> Underestimation of the theme of love has brought many
> f our film men to the point where they overlook a number
> f problems of immense, primary social importance. A lag
> most possible precisely in questions of love, the family,
> nd everyday existence, where people are not directly part
> f a larger group. It often happens that, at his work, a man
> eems to be advanced—he is both a Stakhanovite and an
> ctive person in the community—but in his family he de-
> aands a rigid domestic regime, he is egotistic and coarse
> r has a thoughtless, irresponsible attitude. We must al-
> ays remember that, sooner or later, this will affect all his
> vorking and public life and every moral aspect of the
> aan. The sphere of private life must not be forgotten. It
> essential to mobilize all resources of the cinema, includ-
> ıg such genres as comedy and satire, which scourge with
> umor and sear with fire the bourgeois survivals not only
> a the people's public, but in their private life.[2]

The protests thus fall in line with the requirements
or Soviet discipline in the service of the Soviet state.
'he new principles of sexual morality, which are to
eaffirm the *autonomy* of the erotic relationships as
gainst their subordination to the work relationships

[2] M. Shmarova, "On Those Who Do Not Love to Talk
bout Love," in *Current Digest of the Soviet Press*, V, No.
8 (June 13, 1953), 27 (translated from *Sovetskoe Iskusstvo*
[Soviet Art], May 6, 1953). See also *Current Digest of the
oviet Press*, V, No. 25 (August 1, 1953), 17 f.

and values of the "larger community," actually pr
claim the need for a more harmonious accommodatic
of the former to the latter. Love is to become a nece
sity rather than the reflex of freedom in the realm ·
necessity. The law of value, which, according to Mar
regulates the exchange relations between commoditie
is admitted to govern also the relations between tl
individuals. This is most brutally expressed by
woman whose talk at the Second Collective Farm
Congress was quoted by Stalin:[3]

Two years ago there was no bridegroom for me—ι
dowry! Now I have 500 labor days, and the result is:
cannot rid myself of would-be suitors who say they wa·
to marry me. But now I shall look around and make n·
choice.

The fusion of economic and moral values is certain
not a distinguishing feature of Soviet ethics. It mak·
apparently little difference whether the "dowry"
counted in labor days or in stocks, securities, re·
estate, but, according to Western standards, such f·
sion is considered as amoral and is covered up b
ideological commitments. In Soviet ethics, the "ideolo·
ical veil" is much thinner, is almost nonexistent; lo·
and work efficiency are made to go together qui·
well. The societal conditions of love are brought in·
the light of consciousness and of political regulatio·
This is shocking to Western ethics, and the loss
really great: it affects the most cherished images an·
ideals of Western culture. As Wolfson puts it:

In the conditions of socialism, [the theme of Romeo an·
Juliet] has outlived itself. Socialist society offers no scof

[3] According to S. Wolfson, in *Changing Attitudes in Sovi·
Russia: The Family in the U.S.S.R.*, ed. by Rudolf Schlesing·
(London, Routledge & Kegan Paul, 1949), p. 292 (quoted fro·
Wolfson's *Socialism and the Family*).

for the tragic collisions which are produced by capitalism where social conditions prevent the union of lovers, their association in marriage and the family.[4]

The statement reveals more than what its crudity suggests. The story of Romeo and Juliet certainly depends on the "social conditions which prevent the union of the lovers"—as do the stories of Tristan and Isolde, Don Juan, Madame Bovary, Anna Karenina. But these social conditions define not only the unhappiness but also the happiness of their love because they create the dimension in which love has become what it is: a relation between individuals which is antagonistic to the *res publica* and which draws all its joy and all its pain from this antagonism. If Tristan and Isolde, Romeo and Juliet, and their like are unimaginable as healthily married couples engaged in productive work, it is because their (socially conditioned) "unproductiveness" is the essential quality of what they stand for and die for—values that can be realized only in an existence outside and against the repressive social group and its rules. The more this love obeys its own laws, the more it threatens to violate the laws of the social community. Western civilization has recognized this conflict and made it an essential element of its ethics. Law stands against law, value against value—there is no moral decision as to which law shall prevail. Two value systems, two ethics, exist side by side, each in its own right—and each is to assert its own right. The dual morality pertains not only to the erotic loyalty which Western ethics celebrates, but also to other loyalties when group conflicts with group, cause with cause, tradition with tradition. Antigone is right against Creon as Creon is right against Antigone; the revolution is right against

[4] *Ibid.,* p. 300.

the status quo as the status quo is right against the
revolution. By sustaining each of the conflicting parties in its own right, the dual morality has justified
individual and group aspirations which transgress the
restrictive social order; the end of the dual morality
would mean the end of an entire period of civilization.

With the conquest of the erotic danger zone by the
state, the public control of individual needs would be
completed. Effective barriers would have been erected
in the very instincts of man against his liberation. If
and when the second phase is reached with the distribution of the social product according to individual
needs, these needs themselves will be such that they
perpetuate "spontaneously" their political administration. As long as the *res publica* is not the *res* of the
individuals who are its members and citizens, the
harmonization of private sexual morality with political
morality, with the *res publica* must be repressive. The
best it can achieve is probably a higher degree of
rationality in ethics, for example, by reduction or
avoidance of conflicts, of neurosis, of private, personal
unhappiness. This may be a goal worth striving for,
provided happiness does not mean a state of mental
and psychical impoverishment. If the harmonization
succeeds within the framework of authoritarian administration, it would only add one decisive dimension
—that of erotic needs—to the administered social
needs. The development of harmonious love relations
would become part of the "science of consumption"
which looms on the horizon. A very frank statement to
this effect was made by S. G. Strumilin at the conference of the Economics Institute in June, 1950:

Before speaking about distribution according to needs,
the needs being referred to must be clearly defined. The
needs of the members of the communist society are the

needs of educated, cultured people who do not abuse their opportunities of obtaining consumers' goods. A science of consumption is already being created now. An Institute of Nutrition, which studies rational norms of nourishment, exists in the USSR. People's requirements under communism will be extremely diverse and individual, but on an average there must be a gravitation toward fixed norms which would completely satisfy the needs of socially developed people.[5]

[5] *Voprosy Ekonomiki* (Problems of Economics), 1950, No. 10, as translated in *Current Digest of the Soviet Press*, III, No. 2 (February 24, 1951), 7.

12

ETHICS

AND PRODUCTIVITY

It is noteworthy that some of the most significant
features of Soviet ethical philosophy long predate the
Stalinist period. The repressive and rigid morality of
this period is usually sharply contrasted with the
licentious twenties, when sexual morality was factually
and legally free to a degree unknown in previous history. The contrast is partly justified: the "heroic
period" of the Russian Revolution had quite different
ethical as well as political values. However, as the two
periods share certain long-range objectives of socialism
in one country and orbit, so they do certain political
elements of morality. Kollontai, who is considered as
the representative spokesman of revolutionary sexual
morality, sees in childbearing and child raising a mode
of "productive labor," and brands the prostitute as a
"deserter from the ranks of productive labor." [1] The
antagonism between private and public morality,
which Kollontai regards as characteristic of bourgeois ethics, is in her ethical philosophy to be recon-
ciled by "social feelings" which could not be generated

[1] *Prostitutsiia i mery bor'by s nei* (Prostitution and the
Measures of the Struggle Against It) (Moscow, Gosudarstven-
noe Izd., 1921), pp. 22-23.

by the individualist morale of bourgeois society. In
socialist society, the "collective" has become a reality
which "excludes any possibility of the existence of
isolated, self-enclosed family cells." [2] But already at
that time, the new morale was that of a work collective
rather than of a community of free individuals. Productivity, "development of the productive forces," is
then and now the ethical value which is to govern the
personal as well as the societal relationships.

The ethical connotation of the term "productivity,"
or "productive," refers, since the formation of the
"capitalist spirit," to the output of material as well as
cultural goods with a market value—goods which
satisfy a social need. Marx, who maintained that there
was a necessary correlation between growing productivity and impoverishment under capitalism, expressed
the repressive character of this notion of productivity
by reserving the term "productive" only for labor
creating surplus value, and designating all other modes
of labor, including independent creative intellectual
work, as "unproductive." The discrepancy between
social and individual needs, social and individual productivity, must, according to Marxian theory, prevail
as long as social production is not collectively controlled by the individuals whose labor produces the
social wealth. Short of this revolution in the mode of
production, the discrepancy will remain: what is good
for society and for the state, is not necessarily good
for the individual. And by the same token, as long as
the state remains a superimposed independent power,
personal relationships cannot be dissolved into a *res
publica* without remodeling them according to the
repressive needs of the latter. Under such conditions,
the output of children is indeed productive in the same

[2] *Ibid.*, p. 22.

sense as is that of machine tools, and a loving husband and father is "good" in the same sense as is an efficient factory worker.

The subordination of individual morality to the development of the productive forces was greatly strengthened by the changes in Soviet ethics during the Stalinist period, i.e., by the restoration of a rigid, disciplinarian, authoritarian morality in the early thirties. The facts are well known and may just be recalled: tightening of the marriage and divorce laws; reemphasis on the family and its responsibility; praise of "productive" sexual relations; reintroduction of authoritarian education, and so forth. However, it is not the philosophical content of Soviet ethics that has changed, but rather its social content, namely, the level and scope of industrialization and the international framework within which industrialization takes place. With the first Five-Year Plan, the Soviet Union entered the long-range economic, political, and strategic competition with the advanced countries of the West, while the "end of capitalist stabilization" failed to produce a "rise in the revolutionary tide": isolation and conflict rather than an international spread of socialism seemed to be the prospect.[3] The reestablishment of authoritarianism in ethics was clearly part of the general tightening of controls—part of the mental and physical preparation for war, toil, and discipline.

But if the elimination of libertarian ethics belongs to the requirements of primary industrialization, why does the struggle against these ethics continue *after* the creation of the industrial base, with growing productivity and social wealth? Surely the Stalinist policy of totalitarianism has paid off: the use of formerly

[3] See Part I, pp. 35 ff.

denounced methods of "capitalist industrialization" (rigidly enforced labor discipline, long working day, "scientific management," directorial authority, piece wage and bonus system, competitive profitability) have enabled the Soviet economy to "telescope" several stages of industrial development into two decades. However, the Soviet system, like its counterpart, is self-propelling in the sense that continuous growth of labor-productivity and continuous rationalization become the inherent mechanisms which keep the system going. At the same time, the continued existence of the "capitalist environment" and the maintenance of the preparedness economy also make the centralized control of individual needs self-propelling—even though the rate of progress allows relaxation. Soviet ethics testifies to the conflict between increasing productivity and wealth on the one hand and the social need for toil and renunciation on the other. The greater the possibility of using the former for satisfying individual wants and enhancing individual liberty, the greater the need for minimizing the contradiction without weakening the driving power which propels the system. As industrialization progresses and economic competition with the West becomes more imperative, terror becomes unprofitable and unproductive. It is no durable substitute for the productive and rational coordination which a highly developed industrial society requires; these requirements must be injected into the individuals and become their own moral values. What could be left free from institutionalized control and to the pressure of external forces and circumstances during the "heroic period" of the Revolution, what was implemented by terror during the Stalinist period, must now be normalized and made a calculable resource in the moral and emotional household of the individuals.

Morality, in the form of an efficient organization of values guiding individual behavior inside and outside the plant, farm or office, assumes decisive significance as an integral part of progressing rationalization. Thus it is only an apparent paradox that Soviet ethical philosophy continues to taboo—although in a very different form—the libertarian ideas of the revolutionary period at a stage when their realization seems more logical than at the stage of extreme scarcity and weakness.

But with growing productivity and spreading industrialization, international competition is intensified. Within the Soviet state, shortage continues and demands intensive mobilization. While sexual morality has to be sustained and the sexual emancipation of women has to be restricted, female *labor power* must be emancipated beyond the traditional restrictions. According to Soviet ethics, one of the highest values which elevates communist morality over bourgeois morality is the abolition of patriarchal domination and the establishment of equality between the sexes. Soviet spokesmen do not conceal the economic rationale for the new ethics of equality. In a representative justification of Soviet policies in connection with the antiabortion legislation of 1936, Wolfson discussed the emancipation of women in the Soviet Union chiefly from the point of view of the emancipation of female labor productivity. "Socialist society has created conditions in which the work of rearing and educating children leaves woman a chance of combining her maternal functions and duties with active, productive and social work." [4] He pointed out that "the composition of

[4] Quoted from *Socialism and the Family*, in *Changing Attitudes in Soviet Russia: The Family in the U.S.S.R.*, ed. by Rudolf Schlesinger (London, Routledge & Kegan Paul, 1949), p. 283.

skilled labor in the U.S.S.R. has been sharply modified
towards an equalization of female with male labor,
and he regards as the "most interesting point" the fact
that "Soviet women have gained and continue to gain
in those branches of industry which are closed to
women in capitalist society." As an example he mentioned the high rate of female labor in the mining and
metal industries.[5] The equality of women is not confined to the field of manual labor. "Many women oc-
cupy an honored place in the ranks of innovators of
industry, transport, and agriculture, and of scientific
and cultural figures"; they "participate actively in the
management of the Soviet state." [6] Here, Soviet society
has probably surpassed the older industrial countries
—but until the growing productivity is controlled by
the individuals themselves, the economic and cultural
emancipation of women gives them only an equal
share in the system of alienated labor.

It thus appears that the methodical increase in human productivity is mainly an increase in "abstract"
labor power, whose value is measured in terms of the
calculated social need. The distinctions adhering to
the concrete work of the individuals are reduced to
this common denominator (which allows for a whole
system of quantifiable differences, expressed in the
large wage differentials). For the individuals, this
means training for *technical* productivity: the social
need is chiefly expressed in scientifically organized and
rationalized labor time. In Part I of this study, we have
stressed the policy of using whatever working time

[5] *Ibid.*, p. 287.
[6] I. S. Kon, *Razvitie lichnosti pri sotsializme* (The Development of Personality under Socialism) (Leningrad, Vsesoiuznoe
obshchestvo po rasprostraneniiu politicheskikh i nauchnykh
znanii, 1954), p. 16.

may be saved for universal vocational education.[7] Such education tends to develop the individual as an all-round technical instrument (with a highly developed technical intelligence). To be sure, vocational training is to be supplemented by an ever better education for "higher culture"—the technical and political individual is to be the cultured individual. But the same historical trend which establishes the predominance of technological rationality within a repressive political system also vitiates the efforts to rescue the ethics of higher culture. The latter was the product of a civilization in which the ruling groups were genuine leisure classes; their "unproductive" existence (in terms of socially necessary labor) provided the cultural climate. In other words, "higher culture" depended on the institutionalized and ethically sanctioned separation of intellectual from manual labor. The values of the "personality" were not supposed to be and could not be practiced "on the side": they were meant to shape the entire individual existence. In contrast, industrial civilization has progressively reduced the distinction between manual and intellectual labor by subjecting the latter to the values of commodity exchange, and has progressively denied the ethical value of an "unproductive" leisure class. Deprived of its social basis for resistance, culture has become a cog in the machine—part of the administered private and public existence.

The ethics of productivity expresses the fusion of technological and political rationality which is characteristic of Soviet society at its present stage. At this stage, the fusion is clearly repressive of its own potentialities with respect to individual liberty and happi-

[7] See especially pp. 165 ff. above.

ness. Freed from politics which must prevent the
collective individual control of technics and its use for
individual gratification, technological rationality may
be a powerful vehicle of liberation. But then, the
question arises whether the ethics of productivity does
not contain tendencies pushing beyond the restrictive
political framework. The question clearly parallels the
one asked in Part I of this study: there,[8] we suggested
that, under the condition of international "normalization," the development of the productive forces in the
Soviet system may tend to "overflow" its repressive
regimentation and vitiate possible political countermeasures designed to perpetuate regimentation. Now
the question arises whether there is any corresponding
trend in the development of individual productivity
The latter is, of course, part of the former, but as such
it is a subjective factor whose laws of motion remain
its own even if they are "given" from outside (by the
state or by the society). Does the development of
individual productivity as technical productivity perhaps tend to overflow its political direction—and
limitation? Any attempt even at a preliminary answer
would involve a sociological and psychological discussion far beyond the framework of this study
However, because of the importance of the question
for the evaluation of prospective Soviet developments
we venture to offer some suggestions.

One fact seems to be of foremost significance: in
Soviet society, there seem to be no *inherent* forces
which resist accelerated and extensive automation—
either on the part of management or on the part of
labor. The transfer of socially necessary and unpleasant
work from the human organism to the machine is
therefore bound to progress rather rapidly—the more

[8] See especially pp. 169 ff.

so since it is one of the most effective weapons in the competitive struggle with the Western world. Naturally, the saving of human energy thus achieved is largely cancelled in its liberating effect by the repressive usage of technology: length of the working day, speed-up methods, production of waste, and so forth. It is this usage of technology which makes for its dehumanizing and destructive features: a restrictive social need determines technical progress. Any reorganization of the technical apparatus with a view to the best possible satisfaction of individual needs presupposes a "redefinition" of the social need which determines technology. In other words, the truly liberating effects of technology are not implied in technological progress per se; they presuppose social change, involving the basic economic institutions and relationships.

Would the nationalization of the economy perhaps enable Soviet society to skip, as it were, this stage of *social* change and require only *political* change, i.e., transfer of control from above to below while retaining the same social base (nationalization)?[9] The prospects for such a development are linked to the international balance of power. It is precisely the international situation (of "coexistence") which enforces accelerated and extensive automation in Soviet society. As long as this international situation prevails, technological rationality tends to militate against the restrictive political rationality and to drive the latter toward liberalization on the established base.

[9] The distinction between social and political change is, of course, very precarious, but here it might serve to underline the difference between a development involving a change in the economic structure of society (for example, from private enterprise to nationalization or socialization) and changes within an established economic structure.

The technological rationality also contains an element of playfulness which is constrained and distorted by the repressive usage of technology: playing with (the possibilities of) things, with their combination, order, form, and so forth. If no longer under the pressure of necessity, this activity would have no other aim than growth in the consciousness and enjoyment of freedom. Indeed, technical productivity might then be the very opposite of specialization and pertain to the emergence of that "all-round individual" who looms so large in Marxian theory—a theory which, in its inner logic, is based on the idea of the completed rationalization of necessary labor, on the truly technical administration of things.

Needless to say, the present reality is so far removed from this possibility that the latter appears as idle speculation. However, the forces inherent in a systematically progressing industrialization are such that they deserve consideration even if the strongest political forces seem to arrest or suppress them.

13

THE TREND OF
COMMUNIST MORALITY

We have suggested that the common requirements of industrialization make for a high degree of similarity between the featured values of "bourgeois" and Soviet ethics; such similarity appears in the work morality as well as in the sexual morality. Soviet ethical philosophy itself takes cognizance of this relation between the two antagonistic systems by claiming that the ethical values which were vitiated by bourgeois society are being realized in Soviet society—that what had to remain an ideology in the former could become a reality in the latter. The claim of Soviet ethics that, in the Soviet Union, ethical principles govern reality rather than ideology may be just as easily disputed as similar claims in the West. But in spite of all similarity, the question would still be open whether, from the social function of Soviet ethics, a different prospect of development may be inferred. The technical-economic base of Soviet ethics per se does not "prescribe" any such prospects: it makes for the affinity as well as for the fundamental difference between the systems. The common requirements of industrialization may define the affinity; the essentially

different mode of industrialization may generate the
essential difference behind the apparently identical
values.

When we now try to identify the prospective direction of Soviet ethics, we take again the illuminating
statement on Romeo and Juliet as a starting point.
The statement proclaims the passing of the bourgeois
individual by his fulfillment in the *res publica* and
thereby the passing of the autonomous "subject"
which, as *ego cogitans* and *agens,* was to be the
beginning and the end of Western culture. In the
telescoped Soviet scheme, the dissolution of the
autonomous "bourgeois" individual would correspond
to the latest stage of the prevalent industrial civilization, where mass production and mass manipulation
lead to the shrinking of the ego and to the administrative regulation of his material and intellectual needs.
The coordination between private and public existence,
which, at the postliberal stage of Western society,
takes place largely unconsciously and behind the backs
of the individuals, occurs, in the Soviet Union, in the
light of a well-trained consciousness and as a publicized program. It is part of the total mobilization of
the individuals for the requirements of competitive
total industrialization. Here, and only here, are the
remnants and relics of preindustrial culture conquered:
the romantic elements of the individual, especially in
erotic relations, which were almost identical with
"unproductive," socially unuseful relations, are made
congruous with and conducive to political, socially
useful work relations. If this indoctrination is effective,
it would mean, to the individual, the loss of the
entire sphere in which his existence was still free
from the needs of the *res publica;* to the state, it
would mean control over one of the danger zones in

which explosive demands and aspirations could be
kept alive. With the passing of the individual, the
ethical values lose their autonomous character, and
this loss is not compensated by transcendental sanc-
tions and promises. Ethics as a philosophical and
existential discipline in its own right disappears.

But the validity of ethics does not necessarily depend
on autonomy or on transcendental sanction. If it did,
civilized society would long since have exploded, for
the autonomous personality and the efficacy of transcendence have become increasingly corroded by the
growth of technological controls. Sanction may indeed
come from the *res publica* instead of being vested in
a transcendental agency or in the moral autonomy of
the individual conscience. However, such sanction
would be ethically binding for the individual (i.e.,
would be more than external or internalized compul-
sion) only if the *res publica,* in its institutions, were
to protect and promote a truly human existence for
all individuals. Ethics may indeed be political in
substance. Nor is it obvious that an effective system
of overtly political ethics must necessarily result in
a totalitarian state of robots. The pattern of behavior
which Soviet ethics envisages would presuppose that
human existence as well as society is rebuilt: the
"bourgeois individual," whose substance is to a great
extent apart from the *res publica* and whose needs are
apart from the social need, would give way to an
individual who is an integral part of the *res publica*
because *his* needs are at the same time social needs.
Theoretically and historically, such a development
is not impossible: political philosophy has described
it as "community" (*Gemeinschaft*) against "society"
(*Gesellschaft*), as the ideal "Polis," or, in Hegelian
terms, as the harmony of the universal and the

particular; its interpretation in Soviet ethics makes use of the Marxian idea of classless society as the association of "all-round individuals." In all these theories, the realization of such a harmony between the ethical and the political values presupposes a free and rational organization of social labor, that is, the disappearance of the state as an independent power over and above and against the individuals; whereas Soviet ethics fuses ethical and political values in and for a state which wields independent power over the individuals. As long as this situation prevails, the new ethics will continue to function as a subservient instrument for the primary social objective of the state, that is, in the present period, the objective of total industrialization.

However, even at this stage, where Soviet ethics merely seems to recapture and "catch up" with the initial function of "bourgeois ethics," the different social basis of the former does not preclude a different trend of development. Once firmly established, the basic societal institutions enforce and perpetuate the morality which their effective functioning demands. In the Soviet case, this process is not left to the slow but almost automatic impact of the institutions on individual behavior and values—rather, it is systematically directed by the political agencies. But this does not arrest the dynamic according to which the people thus conditioned must in turn influence the development of the conditioning system. No matter how thoroughly they are controlled and how deeply they are conditioned, they perform the necessary labor which reproduces the controlled society. Thus, no matter how "abstract" and "general" this labor may be, they remain the ultimate "productive force." We have suggested that the reemphasis on the "bourgeois values" in the construction of socialism recaptures that stage of ethics where the state relies on the "introjection" of the socially required values rather than on their extraneous imposition, on "spontaneous" reproduction of ethical behavior rather than on terroristic enforcement. But here the "human material" with which Soviet ethics works militates against a mere repetition of the process of "bourgeois ethics."

In the Western tradition, the introjection of ethical values took place in and with the "individual": his emancipation from older traditional economic, political, and ideological bonds was the precondition for the efficacy of the process. Man's *separation* from the state, from the community, from custom and tradition, his *antagonistic* relation to them as well as to the new powers and institutions was to be prerequisite to his moral autonomy, to the spontaneous, internal elaboration and reproduction of ethical values. Only on such ground could introjection become genuine internalization, that is, demands of the individual's own conscience and faith. Their validity is thereby greatly strengthened. They do not appear as imposed upon the individual from outside but rather as flowing from the individual's own ideal nature, sanctioned not by force but by universally valid ethical laws, and obedience to them tends to become instinctual and almost automatic. Duty, work, and discipline then serve as ends in themselves, no longer dependent on rational justification in terms of their actual necessity. Renunciation becomes an integral part of the individual's mental household (part of his constitution, as it were), transmitted from generation to generation through education and the social climate; it does not have to be enforced continually by specific political and economic measures. However, in Soviet society, this process from the beginning is counteracted by the politicalization of ethics, by the absorption of the individual into the *res publica*. The externalization of ethical values allows only for a very low degree of internalization. With the dissolution of the traditional substance of the individual, the basis of internalization is undermined. All ethical values are systematically referred to the requirements of Soviet society: the specific situation of this society, and the objectives and needs of the Soviet state are to validate moral norms. This reference, and this mode of validation is made explicit and perpetually brought to consciousness.

We have tried to show that the political externalization of ethics is ultimately guided by an absolute, i.e., communism, and thus distinguished from pragmatistic relativism. But the absolute standard pertains ultimately to the goal toward which society is to move—not to the moral (and technical) instrumentalities for attaining the goal. No matter how close the latter are identified with the former, the moral norms are not ends in themselves; they aim at the future, and they obtain their sanction only from the societal norms formulated for the future by the state and its organs. Thus, toil as such is not a value, but only toil *for socialism and communism;* not all competitive behavior but only *socialist* competition; not property but only *socialist* property; not patriotism but only *Soviet* patriotism, and so forth. To the individual, this makes no difference as long as he has no choice and as long as the state defines what socialism and communism are and enforces the definition. However, the weakness of internalization impairs the social cohesion and the depth of morality.

Soviet ethics is rationalistic to an extent which may

endanger its stabilization at the desired level. In the first part of this study,[1] we have stressed the magical and ritual elements in Soviet Marxism. In this connection, we have suggested that even these apparently irrational elements operate in the service of the overriding rationality of the system. Its rationalism is inherent in the methodical orientation of moral norms on the "absolute" communist goal, which is in turn rationally defined in verifiable terms. Whether the working day is reduced to five hours and less or not, whether the individual's free time is really his or not, whether he must "earn his living" by procuring the necessities of life or not, whether he can freely choose his occupation or not—all these can be verified by the individuals themselves. No matter how regimented and manipulated the latter may be, they will know whether communism thus defined is a fact or not. Here lies the decisive difference between Soviet social philosophy on the one hand, and fascist and nazi on the other. The latter center around essentially a-rational, pseudonatural entities such as race, blood, charismatic leadership. No matter how rational the actual organization of the fascist and nazi state may have been (the total mobilization and the total war economy in Germany belong to the most efficient performances of modern industrial civilization), this state itself was irrational in its historical function; that is to say, it arrested the development of the material and cultural resources for human needs and organized them in the interest of destructive domination. Its inherent goal constituted the historical limit of the fascist state. In contrast, Soviet rationalism does not stop at the instrumentalities but extends to the direction and goal of social organization. Marxian

[1] See Chap. 3, especially pp. 71 ff.

doctrine provides the conceptual link. The definition
of communism in terms of a production and distribution of social wealth according to freely developing
individual needs, in terms of a quantitative and qualitative reduction of work for the necessities, of the
free choice of functions—these notions certainly appear to the unrealistic in the light of the present state
of affairs. But in themselves they are rational; moreover, technical progress and the growing productivity
of labor make evolution toward this future a rational
possibility.

The question whether or not the structure of the
Soviet regime precludes the future realization of the
possibility has been discussed in the first part of this
study.[2] There we have suggested that the continued
promulgation and indoctrination in Marxism may
still turn out to be a dangerous weapon for the Soviet
rulers. Thus far, the regime has tried to reconcile
ideology and reality by justifying its basic policy in
Marxian terms. The repressive morality canonized
during the Stalinist period is said to express the
objective requirements of the first phase, that is, the
construction of an adequate socialist base. The ethics
of work and leisure discipline, of competitive patriotism in love and toil—the entire morality of political
Puritanism—is supposed to conform to the stage of
socialism which was compelled by scarcity to evaluate
individual behavior according to its socially useful
performance. The ethical rationale is identified with
the sociological rationale.

If this identification, which is essential to the Soviet
ideology, is to be maintained, long-range changes
in the development of society must be accompanied
by changes in the ideology: the repressive morality

[2] See Part I, Chap. 6.

must be reduced with the progressive reduction of scarcity. In the first part of this study, we have proposed that continued growth in productivity under circumstances of long-range "peaceful coexistence" would tend to such reduction. If the Soviet regime cannot or does not wish to relax correspondingly the repressive morality, it would become increasingly *irrational* according to its own standards. This irrationality in turn would tend to weaken the moral fiber of Soviet society. The whole indoctrination was focused on the rationality of the objectives in the individual as well as general interest; faith in this rationality seems to have been a decisive element in the popular strength of the regime. Here the limits of internalization, which seem to be inherent in the prevailing structure of Soviet ethics, may prove to be decisive. Its values are not autonomous since they are in the last analysis validated by an "external" political goal. Only thoroughly internalized ethics can in the long run operate with *autonomous* values, and only a high degree of ethical *autonomy* can in the long run sustain calculable and durable ethical behavior reasonably independent of the vicissitudes of individual existence. Only on such ground can the individual be made morally shockproof against socially required sacrifices, injustices, and inequalities which appear as irrational. The political rationality of Soviet ethics militates against such moral shockproofing of the individual and sustains the idea that the potentialities for human development should grow in accord with the growing social productivity of Soviet society. Ideological pressure thus seems to tend in the same direction as technical-economic pressure, namely, toward the relaxation of repression. To be sure, ideological pressure and even the weakening of the established morality are not per se a serious threat to a regime which has at its disposal all the instruments for enforcing its objectives. However, substantially linked with the economic and political dynamic on an international scale, these forces, though unformed and unorganized, may well determine, to a considerable extent, the course of Soviet developments.

INDEX

VINTAGE RUSSIAN LIBRARY